Twelve Stones

Tools for A Young Woman's Journey

Estitia Stone

Scriptures taken from the Holy Bible, New International Version®, NIV®. Copyright © 1973, 1978, 1984, 2011 by Biblica, Inc.™ Used by permission of Zondervan. All rights reserved worldwide. www.zondervan.com The "NIV" and "New International Version" are trademarks registered in the United States Patent and Trademark Office by Biblica, Inc.™

Copyright © Estitia Stone, 2017
All Rights Reserved

ISBN 978-0-692-94716-6

Book Cover designed by: Jesh Art Studio

Without limiting the rights under copyright reserved above, no part of this publication may be reproduced, stored in or introduced into a retrieval system, or transmitted, in any form or by any means (electronic, mechanical, photocopying, recording, or otherwise), without the prior written permission of both the copyright owner and the above publisher of this book.

I dedicate this book to my future Olympian, my only daughter, Emani. May this book serve as a fundamental guide to you and all young women around the world.

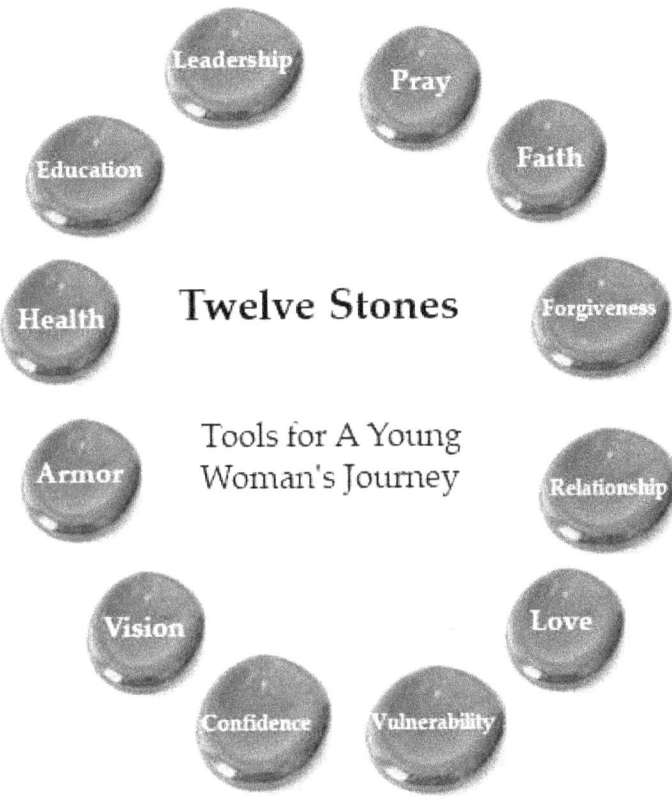

Table of Contents

Introduction 9
December 2, 2014... 11
The Next Day 14
Twelve Stones 16
Tool of Prayer 20
    Say Yes 29
Tool of Faith 34
    Praise & Worship.. 37
    Courage... 38
    Take That Leap Of Faith 40
The Tool of Forgiveness 44
    Great Techniques To Help You Keep Calm....................... 46
Tool of Relationship.. 54
    Friends 55
    Family 59
    Coworkers 60
    Networking 61
    Acquaintances.. 63
    Enemies... 65
    Submission and Authority 65
The Tool of Love.. 70
    Loving Yourself First 70
    Unconditional Love... 76
    Changing Lives Through My Testimony........................... 77
The Tool of Vulnerability 82
    Bonus Tool of Resilience.. 85
The Tool of Confidence 88
    Confidence Boosters... 92
Tool of Vision... 96
    What Is Your Purpose?... 97
    Second Guessing... 100
    Greatness in You And I 100
The Tool of Armor 104
    The Whole Armor of God 105
The Tool of Health/ Wellness 114
    Mental Health 120

- Mental Health Facts 121
- Some Signs of People Struggling: 122
- Spiritual Health 122
- The Tool of Education 128
  - High School 130
  - College/Undergrad 132
  - Student Loans 134
  - Student Internship 135
  - Responsibility 137
  - Goal Focused 138
  - Go- Getter 139
  - Our Circle Is What Defines Us 140
  - One Year Goals 142
  - Two Year Goals 142
  - Five-Year Goals 142
- The Tool of Leadership 144
- Scriptures 150
  - Scriptures on Prayer. (NIV), (KJV) 150
  - Scriptures on Faith 150
  - Scriptures on Forgiveness 151
  - Scriptures on Relationship 152
  - Scriptures on Love 152
  - Scriptures on Vulnerability 153
  - Scriptures on Confidence 154
  - Scriptures on Vision 154
  - Scriptures on Armor 154
  - Scriptures on Health 155
  - Scriptures on Education 155
  - Scriptures on Leadership 155
- About the Author 160
- Reference 161

Introduction

Have you ever felt hopeless, confused, misguided, fearful, or continually doubt yourself? Do you wish you could change something about your life or you felt like, if you had this or that life would be better?

Do not worry any longer. I am here to help you and get you started on your journey to success, health, and leadership.

I have been where you are. I felt abandoned, hopeless, and did not know what the next day would bring.

I was once told – "There is more to life then what meets the eye." I did not understand then, but I do now. It is true. Just because life may not be where you want it to be, does not mean that it is never going to happen.

There is more to life than your reality and your story. We all have a story. We all have an opportunity to create our happy ending.

If you want a happy and life fulfilling ending, you must do something about it that changes the outcomes of your current situation.

I had to stop my current situation from being my story and my excuse. No longer will your current situation be the end of your story.

There are resources and tools in this book, in your community, and around the world that will help guide you, and give you the direction needed to be successful. Being in your same shoes, in my youthful years, I knew I could be someone great.

I believed my Head Start teacher, when he told me I could be anything I want to be. But being in a failing school district and in a struggling community, how can a young person begin to dream beyond that?

I did not know how I would get there, but I knew the road would be complicated.

I knew I wanted a college degree, but I did not think I would make it out with a Bachelor's of Science in Criminal Justice and Masters of Public Administration.

Who knew I would graduate with a Master's degree?

Who knew I would accomplish my goals while raising my daughter, as a single parent, while attending undergrad and graduate school.

Things do happen in life – just know that this is only the beginning of your story. You have a bright future ahead of you.

Come on. Let's learn how these twelve tools can help and let's do the work to get there.

Here is my *Young Woman's Guide to Success, Health, and Leadership*.

Through this book, we will introduce the twelve tools I used through my journey, and how it has helped me to become the author and motivator that I am.

Today, I specialize in motivating young women along their journey, and helping them to achieve each goal they set.

I am here for you and you are here for me. Yes, we will learn and grow with each other because it takes a village to raise a great leader.

I welcome myself to your village. As you journey through this guide, it will lead you down a road to a better understanding, of the essential tools and skills needed, while navigating to achieve your goal(s).

December 2, 2014

Let's take a journey back to, December 2, 2014 – a date that changed my life forever. Taking a peak back helps us all stay humble along our journey, as we all grow and prosper.

Now let's go to the months and days approaching December 2014. I was extremely frustrated and felt lost with life. I have always been a girl with many dreams. With my mind running marathons in my head, I struggled to put things into perspective.

The day of December 1, 2014, I sat in my supervisor's office, as I had many days before, looking and searching for answers.

She asked, "What is wrong with you?" as she always had, during my many days of walking around looking and feeling lost from the world. I told her I did not feel like I was doing anything with my life.

I worked with a population of adults and teens diagnosed with severe mental illnesses, who had lost hope. I could not do much about it, except pray for them.

It was completely out of my control. Being a goal driven person, it became challenging for me to continue the work for them.

I said, "continue the work for them," because I was pushing them harder than they were pushing themselves. It was like playing tug-a-war, leaving me feeling helpless and defeated.

At the time, I honestly hated my job and the current situation of my life. I did not feel like I was on the right track, following God's will and seeking to understand my purpose in life.

I was twenty-seven years old then seeking answers as many other young people. I knew people in my life were not going to provide with answers I needed.

As a Christian, I depend on the power of prayer to guide me. I knew it was time to pray. In times like this, you have to shut yourself away- yes away from everyone. Go into your prayer closet, room, or bathroom—wherever you go—and just pray.

That night I went home and prayed hard. I asked God for direction, understanding, patience, and wisdom to fulfill his purpose and serve his people. I can honestly say, that night was life changing.

I never experienced anything like it before. Everything was moving so fast. Information and ideas were developing in my mind. I always wanted to write a book and start a business—way before this particular day, but still, I did not have a clear vision or direction.

That night, God revealed the concept of my book, along with the title. I did not know the path God was taking me down; nevertheless, I knew to trust and believe he was directing me to a place he wanted me to be.

I attempted to go to bed at three o'clock in the morning after finishing my prayer, but I could not fall asleep. The Holy Spirit directed me to read my Bible.

After reading my daily verse from the Bible plan (*God's Gift*; Revelation 4:1–11, King James Version). I continued reading and found myself reading chapters 4–18. I looked up for the time, and it was 4:48 am.

I had a strong desire to continue, I continued reading. After reading the fourteenth chapter in Revelation, I was moved and vowed to God that I wanted to go to Heaven and do right by him.

I advise you to read the book of Revelation. I promise it could change your life forever.

≈≈≈≈≈≈

Revelation 4:1–11, (KJV).

¹ After this I looked, and, behold, a door was opened in heaven: and the first voice which I heard was as it were of a trumpet talking with me; which said, Come up hither, and I will shew thee things which must be hereafter.

² And immediately I was in the spirit: and, behold, a throne was set in heaven, and one sat on the throne.

³ And he that sat was to look upon like a jasper and a sardine stone: and there was a rainbow round about the throne, in sight like unto an emerald.

⁴ And round about the throne were four and twenty seats: and upon the seats I saw four and twenty elders sitting, clothed in white raiment; and they had on their heads crowns of gold.

⁵ And out of the throne proceeded lightnings and thunderings and voices: and there were seven lamps of fire burning before the throne, which are the seven Spirits of God.

⁶ And before the throne there was a sea of glass like unto crystal: and in the midst of the throne, and round about the throne, were four beasts full of eyes before and behind.

⁷ And the first beast was like a lion, and the second beast like a calf, and the third beast had a face as a man, and the fourth beast was like a flying eagle.

⁸ And the four beasts had each of them six wings about him; and they were full of eyes within: and they rest not day and night, saying, Holy, holy, holy, Lord God Almighty, which was, and is, and is to come.

⁹ And when those beasts give glory and honour and thanks to him that sat on the throne, who liveth for ever and ever,

¹⁰ The four and twenty elders fall down before him that sat on the throne, and worship him that liveth for ever and ever, and cast their crowns before the throne, saying,

¹¹ Thou art worthy, O Lord, to receive glory and honour and power: for thou hast created all things, and for thy pleasure they are and were created.

≈≈≈≈≈≈

The Next Day

I spoke about the readings in Revelation the entire day to my supervisor and close family and friends.

I continued reading Revelation. Upon reading Revelation 21:12, the Bible begins to speak of the gates of heaven.

≈≈≈≈≈≈≈

Revelation 21:12, (KJV).
12 And had a wall great and high, and had twelve gates, and at the gates twelve angels, and names written thereon, which are the names of the twelve tribes of the children of Israel:

≈≈≈≈≈≈≈

Heaven's foundation had a great, high wall with twelve angels at the gates. On the gates were written the tribes of Israel. Referencing back to my beginning stages of developing an idea and title for this book.

I referenced the title *Twelves Stones* in representation of the twelve tribes from Israel, who originally removed twelve stones from the bottom of the Jordan River, in the book of Joshua.

The removal of the *Twelve Stones* represents their journey of crossing and departing the Jordan River for future generations to come. The Bible continues to discuss the foundation of heaven.

≈≈≈≈≈≈≈

Revelations 21:14, (KJV).
14 And the wall of the city had twelve foundations, and in them the names of the twelve apostles of the Lamb.

≈≈≈≈≈≈≈

The wall of the city had twelve foundations, and on them were the names of the twelve apostles of the Lamb.

I continued reading and enjoyed every word. The foundations of the city walls were decorated with every kind of precious stone. I thought to myself, "Okay, precious stone, we are getting somewhere."

The next few verses named the twelve precious stones.

≈≈≈≈≈≈

Revelation 21:19-20, (KJV).

[19] And the foundations of the wall of the city were garnished with all manner of precious stones. The first foundation was jasper; the second, sapphire; the third, a chalcedony; the fourth, an emerald;

[20] The fifth, sardonyx; the sixth, sardius; the seventh, chrysolyte; the eighth, beryl; the ninth, a topaz; the tenth, a chrysoprasus; the eleventh, a jacinth; the twelfth, an amethyst.

≈≈≈≈≈≈

I began to get chills through my body, sweating and shaking. I thought to myself, "This cannot be." As I recall, an amethyst is the February birthstone and February 11 is my birthday.

To confirm, I Googled it because, of course, Google knows everything. All I can say is, "Thank you, Lord, my God, you are awesome." The twelfth stone was amethyst.

You are probably thinking, "that does not really mean anything." Well, anytime I receive confirmation in any form, I believe in my heart, I am on the right track on my journey with God. My *Twelve Stones* are all you need to begin, restart, or continue on this journey to greatness.

The meaning of *Twelve Stones* is extensive. Twelve stones have a range of meaningful representations throughout the Bible.

As a gift to young women, I want to give back to my community and the generations to come. I dedicate this book as a guide to young women around the world; especially those born into poverty, often living in single parent households, having low self-esteem, being abused or bullied, and so on.

They need a little extra empowerment, direction, motivation, spiritual growth, and character development, to become powerful women to lead, influence, serve, and uplift future generations of younger women.

Twelve Stones

Twelve Stones are twelve tools dedicated to young women growing and maturing across the country and around the world.

These tools are provided to help direct, empower, motivate, and strengthen young women, while providing them with the tools to deepen and better understand their relationship with God.

This book focuses on my journey to success. I have made mistakes and wish I could go back in time, but I cannot. This will be the only time you ever hear me say, "I cannot," because what I can always do is try.

> "Jump over every hurdle with class and confidence, knowing with God on your side all things are possible."
> —Estitia Stone

Now that is out of my system let's keep moving. I hope this book will assist young women with fighting against the odds of adversity and overcoming obstacles, jump over every hurdle with class and confidence, knowing with God on your side all things are possible.

Think of it as running track. Run the 100 meters, jump over each hurtle, until you cross the finish line.

Throughout your journey, you will have many trials and tests. With each trial comes a storm, and a rainbow follows each storm.

Remember the storm does not always last, and God will never put more on you than you can bear. Yes, we are human and our flesh is weaker than we can ever understand, however, God lives within us. He gives us the strength and power to keep going.

When we say, "Yes" to his will and, "Yes" to his way, "Yes" to all the things and plans he has for us, he will give us his word and strength to fall back on. He will NEVER tempt us so bad that it will destroy us.

≈≈≈≈≈≈

1 Corinthians 10:13, (KJV).
[13] There hath no temptation taken you but such as is common to man: but God is faithful, who will not suffer you to be tempted above that ye are able; but will with the temptation also make a way to escape, that ye may be able to bear it.

≈≈≈≈≈≈

I did not grow up in your typical "society approved" house hold. My mom was striving to make a better life, as a single parent, for my two brothers and I.

During my adolescent journey, I faced many challenges and had to learn to fight against the odds. Thank God for my village, who helped me along the way.

During my journey, there were many days I questioned God. Why could I not be in a home with my father? Why do I have so many baby sitters? My mom worked more than one job.

Why do I spend so many days alone? Why is my brother always running away from home?

I only felt protected around my brother. The many years he was gone, I felt alone and unprotected.

Why am I here on earth, why am I alive?

Some of those same questions followed me into adulthood. I never received an answer, nor did I ever deal with it. Something in me, as a child, kept pushing me to keep going.

I wanted to give up in school. However, I had enough HOPE to keep pushing. Later down the line, I found out that HOPE was really a sense of FAITH.

Hope was really God living inside me. Hope was really the warrior God created me to be.

I knew I wanted to be more than my situation. I wanted more out of life. I wanted to graduate from High School and College. I never thought about Graduate School, but I did that too.

During the end of my adolescent years I had to work hard. My situation was unstable-- we were stable financially and had all the essentials; but I was emotionally unstable, moving from school to school, in a new state and having to make new friends.

I had moments in high school when I wanted to give up on school. I just wanted a different life and different results.

Before moving to Ohio, I never coped with my issues and I never told anyone how I truly felt. I tried living life through other lives and families I admired.

I had many God mothers and friends, whom I would spend the entire weekend and summer vacations with, to avoid returning home to my challenging life. However, as the saying goes, the storm does not last.

Every time I wanted to throw in the towel, God threw it back and reminded me I had to be the light in the world, lead by example, and help other young women.

Pray

Address a solemn request or expression of thanks to deity or other object of worship.

Tool of Prayer

Prayer is our lifeline to God. Prayer is our way of communicating with God. Prayer is simple; a one on one conversation with God.

First acknowledge God. Ask for forgiveness, thank him, and begin talking to him. Talk to him in the same manner you converse with friends. Talk to him when you are going through trials and tests, most importantly when everything is going great.

Without prayer, it is impossible to allow your request for God to be known. It is difficult to build a relationship with God if you are not communicating with him.

It is difficult to have a relationship with anyone if you are not communicating with them.

Yes, God knows our hearts. He knows every desire we have and could hear us without speaking directly to him. But for our request to be known, communication is the most authentic way of talking to God. As stated earlier, it simply starts by opening our mouths and speaking.

Ask for what you want and need. In life, the most important aspect of any relationship, whether it is with our parents, siblings, significant other, family, or friends, is effective communication.

Good communication is key to healthy relationships. Communication is key to success. Everyday messages are misinterpreted and poorly delivered due to miscommunication. I know you have heard the saying, "a closed mouth does not get fed."

That goes for your relationships too, especially with God. Nobody would ever know our needs and wants unless we express them. People, in relationships, operate better when everyone communicates effectively by expressing their needs, wants, concerns, and anything else needed to be communicated. People are not mind readers. Though I would love to have the gift of reading people minds.

Rest assured, God is aware of our needs and wants. Prayer is an act of our faith. It shows we believe in him and that we trust him to provide.

Yes, God will meet every need, without question. It is also important to understand that our wants may or may not be for us, and therefore, they may or may not be honored and/or answered.

Why, because everything we ask for is not meant for us. Sometimes, we ask for things because someone else has it or because we want to look or feel better than the next person. Because you ask for it out of a want, does not mean you will receive it.

It is simple, if it does not align with his plan, it is not for you. Remember God answers our prayers in his own time. God's timing does not always match our expectations. Your answer may be delayed for many days or many years. Only God knows the plan he has for you, and the timing of his delivery.

≈≈≈≈≈≈

Jeremiah 29:11, (KJV).
11 For I know the thoughts that I think toward you, saith the LORD, thoughts of peace, and not of evil, to give you an expected end.

≈≈≈≈≈≈

When all else fails, we are given God's word to fall back on to guide us. When we are going through our trials and tests, we must give him back his word.

Take authority and use the power of prayer. Learn to stand on his word, allow a sense of peace to take over your life.

Ask yourself, how can you stand on his word, if you do not know what his word says? How can you give God back his word if you do not know what his word says? How can we fight with the sword (word) if we do not know what we are fighting with or against?

To stand on his word, it is important to read his word. Take out your bibles daily and read the word. Meditate on it.

We are not always going to be able to quote it, but from experience, believe me it will come to you in time of need.

Talk to him, throw his words back at him, in the time of need or in the mist of the storm. Find a scripture that meets your situation and meditate on it. Concentrate on the word, not what you are going through.

Tell God what he said he would do. He said he would never fail us or forsake us.

≈≈≈≈≈≈

Deuteronomy 31:8, (KJV).

⁸ The Lord himself goes before you and will be with you; he will never leave you nor forsake you. Do not be afraid; do not be discouraged."

≈≈≈≈≈≈

Communicate with God. He is waiting for you to talk to him and make him prove to you that he is God. He is a willing God. He is a powerful God. He is a healer.

He is a teacher, doctor, lawyer – you know the song by Vickie Winans – *As Long as I Got King Jesus, I Do Not Need Nobody Else.*

He is waiting for you to talk to him and pray, so he can do what he promised you he would do.

He promised us he would supply our needs.

≈≈≈≈≈≈

Philippians 4:19, (KJV).

¹⁹ And my God shall supply all your needs according to His riches in glory by Christ Jesus.

≈≈≈≈≈≈

He promised, he would not hold anything back from us that benefits us or brings good to our lives. You have to say "Yes," to his will and walk uprightly.

≈≈≈≈≈≈

Psalms 84:11, (KJV).

¹¹ For the Lord is a sun and shields: The Lord will give grace and glory: no good thing will he withhold from them that walk uprightly.

≈≈≈≈≈≈

He promised us peace.

≈≈≈≈≈≈≈

John 14:27, (KJV).
²⁷ Peace I leave with you, my peace I give unto you: not as the world giventh, give I unto you. Let not your heart be troubled, neither let it be afraid.

≈≈≈≈≈≈≈

And guess what, he must keep his promise.

≈≈≈≈≈≈≈

Psalm 89:34, (KJV).
³⁴ My covenant will I not break, nor alter the things that is gone out of my lips.

≈≈≈≈≈≈≈

God said it, so he must honor his word.

One of God's best promises is the covenant that He would never flood the earth completely again. He gave us a vow in remembrance of his promise, after every storm we see a "rain bow."

≈≈≈≈≈≈≈

Genesis 9:13, (KJV).
¹³ I do set my bow in the cloud, and it shall be for a token of a covenant between me and the earth.

≈≈≈≈≈≈≈

Communication is one of the key factors for building a relationship with God. Our first step using our Tool of Prayer is learning to communicate with God daily.

It is important because it helps bring us closer to him. It helps God understand where we are, in our walk with him. It helps him understand our faith and loyalty to him. God is a jealous God,

≈≈≈≈≈≈≈

Exodus 34:14, (KJV).
[14] For thou shalt worship no other god, for the LORD, whose name is Jealous, is a jealous God:

≈≈≈≈≈≈≈

We give so much attention and entertainment to the people of this world, we forget to spend our time building a relationship with God.

We forget to put aside time to pray. We forget to go into our prayer corners or closets. I know you have seen *The War Room*, if not go rent it or buy.

It is a lifestyle, to take out time throughout your day to pray. Have a conversation with God. Tell him how much you love him, need him, and honor him.

Before getting out of bed in the morning --thank him. Thank him for keeping you throughout the night. Thank him for protecting you and surrounding you with his angels all night. Thank him for peace of sleep and rest.

He did not have to do it.

≈≈≈≈≈≈≈

Proverbs 3:24, (KJV).
[24] When thou liest down, thou shalt not be afraid: yea, thou shalt lie down, and thy sleep shall be sweet.

≈≈≈≈≈≈≈

Tools for Your Journey

Before getting on Facebook, Instagram, Snapchat or any social media outlet, give him thanks. Thank God for his protection, healing, rest and covering.

Before heading out the door, read your daily devotional, scriptures, Sunday school lessons, whatever you have to prepare you, for your interaction, with everyone in your house and outside your door.

Before walking out the door, prepare for your interaction with everyone. It is necessary to have a sound mind and to be kind and loving towards others.

It is easy for many of us to go from 0 to 100 with our attitude. While we are leading by example, we must learn to lead with kindness and love.

You prepare by putting on your armor. Breast plate of righteousness etc. (refer to *Tool of Armor*). You know people are going to try you all day. You know people are petty.

Be prepared and stay in the word. Pray for your friends and family's safety throughout the day.

Pray for the people at your job, in traffic, at school. Pray for your protection to and from throughout the day. Pray for your enemies, because they need love and prayers too.

Ask God to surround your means of transportation with his blood. Surround the work place, the schools, protect the children and students at school with his angels.

Learn how to praise God throughout the day. Throughout the night. Lift him up and give him thanks. On the job or at school. Pray for peace. Pray for understanding, wisdom, and knowledge.

There is plenty we can talk to God about throughout the day. He is waiting to hear from you. Yes, he knows all, but how would he know you believe and trust in him, if you do not communicate with him.

Be vocal, let the devil know he does not consume you. You know who you are, you know who you belong to so TALK TO GOD.

God is ready to move on your behalf. Open your mouth and talk to him. He is ready to meet the need. Believe me, God is anxious to help you, but he wants to know that you trust him to do so.

Never get to a place where you are not talking to God, and making your requests known. Why would you not talk to him? He knows all. He knows your expected end.

Since he already knows what you are going to do, why not ask him for more wisdom, knowledge and understanding?

We do not know everything and there is always room for growth. I have people connected to me that say, "I feel like I ask God for too much. I feel like I do not need anything."

Girl please, you can never have too much. You will never be able to meet any need alone. You are not in control. You do not run your life.

You do not have all that God promised to you. Do you know what he has for you? Do you know your worth? Do you have it all?

I am sure there are places you would like to visit, to have more money, more self-control, more joy, more happiness, more things, more knowledge, more wisdom, and more understanding.

You can NEVER have too much. So why not pursue it? Why not ask? What are you waiting for? Go ahead, open your mouth, and say THANK YOU LORD. Thank you, Lord, for your guidance, peace, love, and happiness.

You are what you say you are. You are what you speak into your life. There is power in the tongue, are you speaking LIFE into your life, or are your speaking death? When the going gets tough, are you saying, "All is well."

When your money gets low and you cannot physically see your riches, are you saying, "I am broke," or are you saying, "I am rich in the Lord."

When you cannot see clearly through the storm, are you casting all your worry and anxiety upon the Lord, or are you trying to handle it yourself.

≈≈≈≈≈≈

1 Peter 5 :7, (KJV).
7 Casting all your care upon him; for he careth for you

≈≈≈≈≈≈

Are you asking God to bind up the devil, or are you trying to cast out the devil yourself? Cry out to the Lord. He is ready and waiting on you. This world is his foot stool there is nothing he cannot do.

≈≈≈≈≈≈

Isaiah 66:1, (KJV).
1 Thus saith the LORD, The heaven is my throne, and the earth is my footstool: where is the house that ye build unto me? and where is the place of my rest?

≈≈≈≈≈≈

The power of the Lord is nothing we can imagine. He sees all and can do all. Who are we to limit him? Who are we to say what he can and cannot do? I can only imagine the humor we entertain God with daily.

I am sure he gets frustrated with us, likewise there are many times he sits back and giggles at us.

When are you going to get tired of running in circles? When are you going to get tired of trying to do it alone? When are you going to get tired of being the head of your life?

It is simple and easy, just give it to the Lord. No, the process is not easy, I tried controlling my life for years. I was that chick who always appeared to have it together, but I was struggling inside.

I was that girl who never asked for help; when I did, nobody was there. I never showed that I needed anyone. So, when I did, I felt as though people were judging me.

When you have it all together and lose it all, people will judge you because, you were the one, who never allowed anyone to see you sweat. Never allowed anyone to see your mishaps. Thank God for growth.

Now I feel like I wear my feelings on my sleeve all the time. I can cry at the drop of a dime, well maybe two dimes. I say this to say, "Let go and let God into your life."

Say Yes

Give God your YES. Giving God your YES means to say YES to his will and his way. Say YES to the things he has for you. YES, to the plans he has for you. YES, to your purpose here on earth and the reason he created you.

Consult with him first, wait for him to answer, then go with his answer. You will know when he says, YES.

He may even give you a clear vision, clear as day. It will most likely come in a dream. You may have developed a relationship with him so great, you will be able to hear him speak to you.

Nonetheless, you will know when he has answered. You will feel at peace with your decision. Everything will fall into place just right. You will have favor with people. Things will run smoothly without forcing it to happen.

Sometimes you will find people are on the same page as you. God will set everything up just right when it is for us. I am not saying you are not going to have to work for it, but when you do, everything will be waiting for you.

Everything will go smoothly for the job you have been praying for; the interview will seem effortless, you may not experience nervousness.

The dream college or university you have been hoping to enroll in, apply, if it is for you everything will go as planned.

Do not limit yourself. Just because it does not look like you qualify, in Jesus' name, it is yours. Dream big, you got this, give it to the Lord, it is yours.

It sounds condescending but, faith without work is dead. Praying without work is dead. You have to do your part too. You cannot sit back and wait without working for something. Who sits back and waits on test results, without putting in the hours studying and completing class work before the test?

Hopefully no one. You have to do your work. Pray, wait, work, wait, pray and do it all over. There is work to do while waiting.

Always end your day and start your day with prayer. End your day and start your day communicating with God. Thank him and ask him for his forgiveness.

Ask him to forgive you, for all the times you said you could not do it. Ask him to forgive you, for all that you have done to work against him, the things you were aware of and the things you were not.

What are you asking God to do in your life?

Tools for Your Journey

Faith

Allegiance to duty or a person.

Tool of Faith

Some may ask, why put the Tool of Prayer before the Tool of Faith? The tool of Prayer is first because it is the purest method for reaching God. Do you stand, on his word, and believe that he is going to answer your prayer? After you have your daily conversation with God, what's next? Do you brush him off, do you forget what you asked?

If you have decided you are going to stand on his word, and believe your prayers will be answered, then you have decided to be faithful and believe God will honor his word and provide.

Because faith without believing is not possible. When you believe, you expect God to provide. When we expect God to provide, the first thing we have to do, with our expectation, is communicate. Communication is through prayer, which allows our needs, and wants to be heard.

Faith without prayer is dead. Why communicate with God and make our request known if we have doubt in our heart he would provide? If we do not trust him, to provide anything, why are we faithful? Why would we waste time praying, if we do not trust God to do what he said he would do?

Prayer and faith work together to deepen our relationship with God. Prayer allows our request to be known and faith shows that we are hopeful that God will meet the need.

≈≈≈≈≈≈≈

Romans 14:23, (KJV).

[23] And he that doubteth is damned if he eat, because he eateth not of faith: for whatsoever is not of faith is sin

≈≈≈≈≈≈≈

Hebrew 11:1, (KJV).

[1] Faith is the substance of things hoped for and the evidence of things not seen.

≈≈≈≈≈≈≈

The practice of faith is remaining hopeful and positive, that the things you asked God for, or the things God said he would do, will come to past.

As we grow spiritually, our faith will grow as well. In the beginning, as babies in Christ, we do not know we have the faith to move mountains. It is hard to understand in the beginning.

As we mature in Christ, and grow in the word, we are then exposed to more of what God has for us, and the things he said he would do for us. If you are not familiar with the word, you will not have a clue, about what is possible or destined for you, in your life.

But as you continue to read the word (bible) and develop a stronger relationship with God (through prayer and obedience), you will begin to trust him more, look for him to meet the need more, and call on him more.

All you need is faith the size of a mustard seed. Are you familiar with a mustard seed? Faith of a mustard seed can move mountains.

≈≈≈≈≈≈

Mathew 17:20, (KJV).
20 *And Jesus saith unto them, Because of your unbelief: for verily I say unto you, if ye have faith as a grain of mustard seed, ye shall say unto this mountain, Remove hence to yonder place; and it shall remove; and nothing shall be impossible unto you.*

≈≈≈≈≈≈

The ultimate outcome of having faith is being set free from danger and suffering; salvation. Being free from hurt, harm, dangers of this world. As we continue to walk this journey with God, and see things happen, our faith will strengthen. We will start to believe God can do bigger and greater things in our lives.

Tomorrow is not promised, but I stand on God's word daily. God promised me, He will keep me, protect me, and direct my paths every day.

≈≈≈≈≈≈

Psalms 91:4-5 (KJV).
4 *He shall cover you with His feathers; and under his wings shalt thou trust: his trust shall be thy shield and buckler.*
5 *Thou shalt not be afraid for the terror by night; nor for the arrow that flieth by day.*

≈≈≈≈≈≈

You should never be afraid of what tomorrow will bring. Put all your trust in the Lord with all your heart. I live for today and I am hopeful that tomorrow will come, and the entire day will be good.

≈≈≈≈≈≈≈

Philippians 4:6, (KJV).

⁶ Be careful for nothing, but in everything by prayer and supplication, with thanksgiving, let your requests be made known to God;

≈≈≈≈≈≈≈

Whatever tomorrow brings was meant to be and was all a part of God's plan. I have no control over tomorrow, so why worry about it. Let go and let God do his works.

Praise & Worship

We all have something or someone we worship and/or praise. Ask yourself, in your everyday life, what are you worshiping and praising? No, we do not all worship the same God. Ask yourself, whatever you are worshiping, is it bringing goodness to your life?

Is it depleting your worries? Is it bringing happiness to your life? Is it uplifting your life? Is it providing an encouraging word? Is it getting you through your trials and tests without failing?

Think about it for a minute. If it is not, then we have to do something about it -- if it is, continue doing what you are doing, because it is working for you.

God has already finished his plan for you and he has sat down. God is watching every day.

He is watching to see who is passing the test, who is praying, who is being obedient, and who is being faithful.

He is also paying attention to people we call fence people. People who sit on the fence, every day, deciding when they want to follow God, or when they want to follow the world.

God is not looking for "fence people."

You cannot have your foot in the world and in the word. Nonetheless, you must make a choice. Serve God or serve the world, but you cannot serve both.

≈≈≈≈≈≈≈

Deuteronomy 30:19, (NIV).
19 This day I call the heavens and the earth as witnesses against you that I have set before your life and death, blessings and curses. Now choose life, so that you and your children may live.

≈≈≈≈≈≈≈

God is a jealous God. You cannot serve two God's.

God has sat down; he is waiting on you. He already created a purpose for you. We discuss this in the *Tool of Vision* chapter.

God has a vision for each one of us. As we seek after him through prayer and reading, he begins to show us more of our destiny.

Courage

≈≈≈≈≈≈≈

2 Timothy 1:7, (KJV).
7 For God has not given us a spirit of fear, but of power, and of love, and of a sound mind.

≈≈≈≈≈≈≈

Having courage is doing things while being afraid, but still moving forward in things that cause the fear.

Fear prevents us from doing anything. Fear prevents us from getting the job done. Fear prevents us from being great. Whatever it is that has you afraid, you must confront it head on.

Let it know you are not afraid, you will conquer with confidence and succeed knowing you gave it your best while trusting God.

We have the power we need to get the job done, to complete the task. As my former supervisor use to say, "Get her done."

Still, we fail ourselves by living in fear and relying on others to protect us, boost us, and give us courage to keep moving. We fail to use faith to help us along the way.

The devil loves to fight against us on this level. He loves to get into our heads, play with our minds and our hearts.

Satan uses our power against us to take over our lives. How does this work? He uses us to be against ourselves. The takeover is real. We are witnesses to it daily.

We allow ourselves to lose hope and sanity, become powerless, and doubt our abilities to be great.

People speak death into their lives – saying what they cannot do or what is impossible. Now how is that? When it is all said, and done, we still have the power God has given us. We must learn to use it.

How can we be courageous? Do anything and everything when we are afraid? Yes, we are not perfect and everyone fears something.

I completely understand and have been where you are: going to new schools, speaking in front of people, giving presentations for work or school, etc.

It all can be scary, but the difference between living courageously and living in fear is not doing anything about it and being stuck in that moment.

We must work at living courageously every day. Deliverance may not take place over night, but every day you can work towards success. Every day you will become stronger in faith and believe everything is going to be okay.

When you are a believer and know who you belong to, you will gain enough faith and confidence to push through.

Do not allow the devil to push you to a place where you live in fear. Fear is what holds us all back. It gets in our heads and keeps us from doing things our heart desires.

It keeps us from taking that first initial step. We have to gain enough faith and courage to take that first step, to begin our journey, to whatever it is you want to accomplish in life.

Take That Leap Of Faith

What is a leap of faith? Google defines leap of faith as *"an act of believing in or attempting something whose existence or outcome cannot be proved"*

Let's break it down further, the act of believing in; means first you have to know that you can do it, get it done and achieve it.

You have to know in your heart, you can accomplish it. Sometimes others believe we can do it, however, we lack faith and confidence, to know for ourselves we can do it.

So much goes on in our head that discourages us from doing anything. We put so much junk in our own mind and heart, we stop ourselves from accomplishing the goal and getting the job done.

We tell ourselves *"oh that is too hard, it takes too much of my time, I do not have the money, I do not have the resources, I do not know how to. I cannot do it."*

Those are all excuses that limit us from being our best, from doing our best and accomplishing our best. My daughter refers to those words as "junk words."

What is our best;

- Anything you put your "all" into.
- Anything you do without coming short of conquering your goal.
- Anything you do until you cannot push any more.
- Going until you reach whatever it is your heart desires.

The only thing that should prevent you from achieving your goal is sickness or injury. But there are athletes that push through that too. So, all excuses are a deterrent that stops you from pushing through.

- Learn to be a pusher and a go getter.
- Learn to fight to the end.
- Learn to motivate yourself.
- Learn to navigate through life setting goals.
- Implement a plan to reach your goal and use tools and resources provided along the way to achieve the goal.

There are people in this world, who love to see us fail, and there are people who love to see us succeed.

I am the person who wants to see you succeed. I have a network of people who aspire the same for you. I want you to succeed and I am here to help. Reach out -- I look forward to hearing from you.

(email: info@estitiastone.com; social media, everywhere, Estitia Stone).

What is your greatest fear? What are you going to do to face it?

Forgiveness

The act of forgiving someone or something. The attitude of someone who is willing to forgive other people.

The Tool of Forgiveness

Forgiveness is not an easy task; however, it is worth a try. Forgiving is probably the hardest part of a relationship. It is not something you master overnight, it takes time and dedication.

You have to work at forgiving others every minute, hour, and day. Once something happens, you should practice forgiving immediately.

Yes, there were times in life I held grudges, stayed angry at people and removed them from my life.

But ask yourself, is it worth all that? Forgiveness should be a daily homework assignment: morning, day, and especially at night. You never want to go to sleep and allow the sun to set with an unforgiven heart.

≈≈≈≈≈≈

Ephesians 4:26-29, (KJV).

[26] *Be ye angry, and sin not: let not the sun go down upon your wrath:*

[27] *Neither give place to the devil.*

[28] *Let him that stole steal no more: but rather let him labour, working with his hands the thing which is good, that he may have to give to him that needeth.*

[29] *Let no corrupt communication proceed out of your mouth, but that which is good to the use of edifying, that it may minister grace unto the hearers.*

≈≈≈≈≈≈

Do not go to sleep angry at someone. Do not give the devil time to play with your heart. Then wake up the next morning, still angry about the same thing and have the same unforgiveness in your heart.

People are oblivious to the things they do to others. Yes, I know most people are aware of their actions, but there are many individuals that are not aware of the way their actions effect people emotionally.

I totally understand your emotions, but since we are not given the right to judge others, we have to forgive and let go.

You are only accountable for what you do to others. You have to answer for your own actions.

Since you are accountable for your actions, take responsibility for your responses and reactions. I had to learn and accept everything does not need a response.

≈≈≈≈≈≈≈

James 1:19-20, (KJV).
[19] *Wherefore, my beloved brethren, let every man be swift to hear, slow to speak, slow to wrath:*
[20] *For the wrath of man worketh not the righteousness of God.*

≈≈≈≈≈≈≈

We all feel ourselves boiling and getting angry inside. What I want you to do is take control of that anger. You have to practice, it is not going to come over night, however, when you start processing your responses, you will be slower to respond.

We cannot keep giving others the power to control our every move. When you feel a situation getting out of control, walk away, go take a breather, go get some fresh air.

Sometimes it helps to count to 10. While counting, it distracts you from what is going on, providing time to cool down.

If 10 is not long enough, count to 100. Counting also is not adding any negative energy to the situation.

Great Techniques To Help You Keep Calm
- Deep breathing (take a deep breath in. Hold it. Slowly release your breath out. Repeat 10 times).
- Take a walk to clear your head.
- Journaling

Write down techniques you would like to use or are currently using to help you calm down.

_____
_____
_____
_____
_____
_____
_____
_____
_____
_____
_____
_____
_____
_____
_____
_____
_____

Think of forgiveness as an everyday task. There is no strategy or way around it, but a way to get pass it.

It is simple, just forgive and let it go. Do not analyze it. Do not think about it. Do not retaliate. Do not seek revenge. Do not give up.

Pray about it, give it to God, and let it go. As soon as you pray and your prayers are genuine, God will soften your heart and you will be able to move on.

I am not saying, you are going to forget it completely. However, when you see that person, you will not feel any anger towards them.

Although you have forgiven and moved on, its ok to remain cordial with one another. Continue to show kindness, love, and have their best interest.

What is the difference between analyzing forgiveness and tackling problems?

Problems are situations regarded as unwelcome or harmful and needing to be dealt with and overcome. Problems are analyzed then tackled. Forgiveness should happen so quickly, you do not have time to analyze and it only entails one solution; letting it go. Forgiveness should be dealt with and overcome as well. However, forgiveness should be done quickly.

≈≈≈≈≈≈≈

Colossians 3:13, (KJV).

¹³ Forbearing one another, and forgiving one another, if any man have a quarrel against any: even as Christ forgave you, so also do ye.

≈≈≈≈≈≈≈

You do not have to sit and analyze forgiveness as you do with problems. You should not have to think about it or dwell on it. You should forgive quickly. As fast as it happens.

I have grown so much using my *Tool of Forgiveness*. We forget many times, people are human and we all make mistakes.

The way that I handled forgiveness in the past was by cutting people out of my life. If I felt someone did not have my best interest or was my biggest enemy; I would clearly walk away from them. I would block them from calling, delete them from my social media accounts and move on without saying a word.

Now that I am deepening my relationship with God and understanding his word; I have a more forgiving and patient heart. I have more empathy and compassion for people.

I cared about others before, but I failed to put in the work, to be more charitable towards them. To cherish means to be kind and tolerable in judging others.

≈≈≈≈≈≈

Colossians 3:14, (KJV).

14 And above all these things put on *charity, which is the bond of perfectness.*

≈≈≈≈≈≈

It is not perfection; however, you're practicing with the intent of being perfect. Your practicing with the intent to be more like God. Our God is perfect in our eyes, he knows all and created all. There is nothing above him. He is God, all by himself.

≈≈≈≈≈≈≈

Ephesians 4:6, (KJV).

⁶ One God and Father of all, who is above all, and through all, and in you all.

≈≈≈≈≈≈≈

As believers, he lives inside us, it makes sense for us to want to be more like him and strive for perfection. We will never be perfect; however, we can live to practice being perfect.

With practice develops growth, which develops a better you. Growing up we were all taught that practice makes perfect. If we do our best, we are perfect in God's eye.

We spend hours practicing and perfecting everything else, we need to take time to spend hours reading the word and softening our hearts for others. We are put on earth to fulfill a purpose.

Part of fulfilling our purpose is serving his people. To serve, we have to have a loving and patient heart. Part of loving and patience, is being charitable. We cannot be charitable with an unforgiving heart.

I am not perfect, but I try my best to be more like God daily. I have a long way to go, but I do know God understands. God cares more about what is in your heart, than what you did yesterday or last night.

Once you repent and ask God to forgive your sins, you are renewed daily. His grace and mercy for you is renewed daily.

Repent and ask God to heal you and clean you out. Ask him to clean out the things that do not belong and strengthen the things in your heart that is more like him. I want you to know that God understands you.

If you are doing your best, honoring his word, and loving his people, you are all good in his eyes.

He loves you. If nobody else loves you, know that God loves you and I love you.

As God forgives us, we practice forgiving others. There is no other way around it. If God provides grace and mercy for us daily, how fair is it to not show the same grace and mercy towards others.

I promise, you will feel so much better forgiving people and moving on from it. We give so much energy towards other people who could care less about us. Most people do not serve a positive impact in our lives.

There are evil people walking around choosing to be foolish. Justifying their actions and offending people over and over. There is more to life than negative people. Everyone does not deserve to be your friend or to be a part of your life.

Everyone is not intended to stay in our lives permanently. The only people you were not able to choose to be a part of your life is your family, just think, everyone else you get to choose.

You choose wisely by praying to God, asking him to connect you to those wonderful people.

There are some amazing God sent people in this world. It is an amazing feeling to be connected to awesome people. I thank God for my awesome village daily. We have a choice to pray, I hope you choose to pray, to allow for God to move on your behalf, and continue to surround you with great people.

Not all wounds are visible - what are some of your invisible wounds you would like to heal from?

Write down steps you would like to take to heal from your invisible wounds.

Tool of Relationship

There is more to a relationship than a husband and wife. Relationships are built through different connections with people. Example of relationships are mother and father and their child(ren); friends; immediate family; extended family; colleagues; neighbors, the list goes on. Relationship building is not easy and will take some work.

As my Pastor James Holloway Jr would say, "relationships matter." Relationships help define our destiny and prepare for our life experiences.

Too many people in my life have expressed their dislike for having close relationships outside their family ties. Many have stated, "I do not need anyone in my life."

This is not a good attitude to have. Ask yourself a question, "Why did God place so many people in the world? Why did he choose to create families, friends, and enemies?"

God created us all to be in relationship with others. To help, encourage, uplift, bring happiness, and to mourn with one another in time of need.

Every person we encounter, is a part of God's plan. Everything is not going to always be peaches and cream in our relationships. Things are going to happen. But remember, relationship building is a two-way street, it takes more than one to put in the work on building and sustaining healthy relationships.

Friends

My friends are the best and entirely count as one of my favorite blessings. I am thankful to have great people in my corner I can truly call a friend. Whenever I call on them, they are always there. I have not always had the will power to ask for help, but even then, they were there. There are many days I wonder what I would do without my girls.

Friends should not be present in your life to bring stress or any other challenges. I think some of our family members bring enough stress into our lives.

Friendships are not always smooth sailing, but for the most part it should bring goodness.

No relationship is perfect. When things happen, you have to be able to resolve the problem.

Yes, things are going to happen and we live and learn, but you can move on and forgive quickly.

≈≈≈≈≈≈

Colossians 3:13, (KJV).

13 Forbearing one another, and forgiving one another, if any man have a quarrel against any: even as Christ forgave you, so also do ye.

≈≈≈≈≈≈

Be even-tempered, content with second place, and quick to forgive an offence. Forgive as quickly and completely as the Master forgives you daily.

When you are even-tempered your less likely to respond negatively or with angry. One person I know, who can relate to being even-tempered, is my God mother. It takes so much for her to lose her cool, to show anger or annoyance, no matter what the cause may be. She's always cool, calm, and collected, no matter what.

To be content with second is ok. You do not always have to be first, it is just a title and it does not define who you are. If you allow the world to define you and forget who created you, who you belong to and whose child you are, you will forever be lost in this world.

Forgiving quickly is not putting much thought into whatever it is that offended you. I know it is hard to do, it is hard for me to do. But with practice, you will begin to see changes in your responses and behaviors towards others.

With God being the only judge of our souls, you cannot get so anxious about everything someone does. Just know it is not them personally, it is their flesh and you cannot win against flesh.

≈≈≈≈≈≈

Ephesians 6:12, (KJV).

12 For we wrestle not against flesh and blood, but against principalities, against powers, against the rulers of the darkness of this world, against spiritual wickedness in high places.

≈≈≈≈≈≈

Let go of situations and begin to allow God to handle it. I know you have heard the saying, "let go and let God." By letting go you start with prayer. You have to begin all and end all with prayer. Talk to God as you would with your friends and family members.

Let him know who offended you and how you feel. I promise you will feel so much better. Be honest with him, because He already knows your heart. I would suggest talking to him before talking to anyone else.

After speaking to God, later when you converse with your friends about it, you will be more at ease and have a better insight on how you feel and what happened.

Many individuals may consider it as gossiping. Gossiping is sharing information about someone that is a secret, or using privileged information as a talebearer or scandalmonger.

Now we all know the difference. The gossipers goal is to make someone look bad and themselves look good. Even if a person means no harm, it is still unjust.

≈≈≈≈≈≈

Proverbs 21: 2-3, (NIV).
² A person may think their own ways are right, but the Lord weighs the heart.
³ To do what is right and just is *more acceptable to the LORD than sacrifice.*

≈≈≈≈≈≈

If we are not spreading lies and secrets about people, it is not considered gossiping. Stop letting people define so much of you. You know right from wrong. You know when you feel right or wrong, in your heart.

When you go to your consoles, those you confide in, state the facts, and speak not so much from what happened, but the way you felt and how you handled it in a positive manner.

Go to the person who offended you. We learn in Matthew chapter 18:15-18 the order of problem solving and how it should be handled.

≈≈≈≈≈≈

Matthew 18:15-18, (KJV).

15 Moreover if thy brother shall trespass against thee, go and tell him his fault between thee and him alone: if he shall hear thee, thou hast gained thy brother.
16 But if he will not hear [thee, then] take with thee one or two more, that in the mouth of two or three witnesses every word may be established.
17 And if he shall neglect to hear them, tell [it] unto the church: but if he neglects to hear the church, let him be unto thee as an heathen man and a publican.
18 Verily I say unto you, Whatsoever ye shall bind on earth shall be bound in heaven: and whatsoever ye shall loose on earth shall be loosed in heaven.

≈≈≈≈≈≈

People would get so much accomplished by going directly to the person who offended them. I had to learn this the hard way. My way of handling conflict was by cutting people off and dismissing them.

Since I went through so much growing up, I did not have much tolerance and patience for people. Thank God for growth and maturity. I am no longer that person.

I now process the information before I put it out. I am more patient with my friends and have learned how to talk things through without arguing.

Before I developed effective communication and problem-solving skills, my friend's offenses made me feel disrespected and I questioned their loyalty as a friend.

I have always felt I was a loyal friend and I had the same expectations for my friends. If I had ever reached a point, in my friendship, where I questioned their loyalty, it was difficult for me to continue in the friendship.

Do not be this way. If you truly love and care for that person, go talk to them. Learn the difference between reacting and responding. Talk to them, maybe they will have a different perception of themselves, and self-evaluate for future reference.

It is hard to solve a problem, if you refuse to express how you feel, and talk about what happened.

To solve problems, we have to be able to state the problem. If we cannot state the problem, then how are we going to solve anything?

God does close doors with people. You cannot take everyone with you, year after year. Yes, it is true, some people are in our lives for a reason, season, or lifetime.

You have to ask God for wisdom and understanding daily. He will provide and direct our paths. We have to ask God for guidance in our relationships as well.

Friendships are built on trust, if you cannot trust your friends, then you cannot be friends, simple as that.

There are people connected to you, God keeps the door open. As bad as you want to close the door on a person, for whatever reason, God will keep firm control over that door and keep it wide open, until he is ready to release you.

Family

Family is everything. September 12, 2016, I buried my dear father. During this weekend, I was reunited with my sisters and all family members on my father's side.

Some family members I had not seen in over 10 years. During our reunion, my heart was filled with love and joy.

Before departing, my daughter expressed she did not want to leave. In my heart, I did not want to leave my family either. I lived for a good time, with my family. It is very important to find and make time to spend with family.

Family is everything. There is a reason and purpose for you to be connected to the people in your family. There is a reason your parents are your parents, siblings are your siblings, and so on. Our families help us prepare for our destiny.

Along with the good, there are problems. Things will not always be perfect within relationships. There will be good days and bad. We have to learn to fight through those bad days. Relationships can be broken in a matter of seconds, but we have to ask ourselves, is it worth it?

Coworkers

Coworkers are just that, people you work with or share duties with. My experience in the working world, is that our coworkers have expectations of us as well. They want to hang out, they want to bond and they want to know what you did last night. You have to be the one who draws a boundary line between friends and coworkers.

It is ok to have a good time with your coworkers. Remember you see them more than you see your family and friends.

I am not saying you have to be best-friends with your coworkers, but you do have to learn to be friendly and a team player. When everyone works well together and gets along, it allows the team morale to stay afloat. It makes a difference in the team.

Coworkers are not meant to bring stress. Find out what your coworkers need and try to live up to their minor expectations. Not the unrealistic expectations, but small ones such as, going to lunch a time or two, being pleasant, making eye contact, speaking, and smiling; just the minor expectations.

There should not be any expectations on: being best friends, going out to parties, gossiping, talking about your relationships outside the job, doing anything that makes you uncomfortable.

Networking

Networking will be one of the most important skills to have that helps establish career success. Networking is defined as the interaction with other people, to exchange information and develop contacts, especially to further one's career.

Networking requires talking and communicating with others. The key to networking is building relationships. Those relationships can take you very far in life.

Every job within my career stemmed from networking. Let's look at a broader spectrum of networking. Networking can help you get a great job, scholarships, internships, employment after college, help with business ventures, mentors, and coaches.

Networking is a simple conversation with likeminded people. Sometimes networking creates an opportunity to learn something new, receive new insight, or new direction.

If you can walk up to any person and have a conversation, you are on the right track. If you do not know how to begin a conversation, it is ok, you have to start somewhere.

You have to be creative sometimes when approaching people. Start off by finding what you have in common. Not every person you encounter, will want to build a relationship that will last a life time, but believe me some will.

Always network with a purpose. If you are at a career fair, start talking to the recruiter about a job you are interested in, or something new you found out about their company.

Reach out to different organizations you are interested in, to see if you can intern or volunteer. It is also a great idea to reach out to people, currently working, in a position, you hope to serve in later in life as you advance. Show interest and research.

When you are done networking, please do not forget their business cards. Always carry a general career business card with you. My friend Victoria taught me this. You do not have to have a specific job on the card, but include information on who you are, and how they can get in contact with you.

Build quality relationships. Yes, you will meet many people. Most of those people you meet you will never see again, or you will never have another conversation. It is not important to introduce yourself to every individual you encounter. Look for the few that you believe have something in common and you can build a relationship.

Those people who impact your life greatly, are the ones you want to keep in your circle, and a part of your journey. I call those people, 'my go to people.' I call, text, email, Facebook, these people monthly.

I have two mentors from college, who mean the world to me. They have been a part of my life, since the first day I started at Bowling Green State University: Mrs. Ashely Benson and Dr. Tiffany Davis.

These two were my back bone in college. They kept me accountable and motivated me to do my best. I made sure I stopped by their offices weekly. I appreciate all that they have done.

With these two in my corner, it created more opportunity for me to succeed. They wrote my recommendation letters, and were my references for all my jobs after college. They wrote my recommendation letters for two colleges -- I got accepted to both.

Our relationship became stronger because I was committed to the few people who were committed to me.

I cannot forget my English professor, Dr. Cynthia Mahaffey. She is still a part of my life as well. Before applying for graduate school, she made sure my personal statements were the best. In the beginning, our relationship was a little rocky.

She did not think I liked her, but once we got to know each other, we created a bond that was unbreakable.

She always told me I was one of her best writers. Just know I passed her class with an "A."

I wish I could have had her as a professor throughout my college experience, however, she only taught writing at the time.

She has also written a few of my recommendations letters. I keep in touch with her mostly through email and LinkedIn. Bowling Green State University has connected me to some awesome people, I thank God for our crossing paths.

You will network with many people who you will only reach out to on a need basis. The relationship will be mutual. I have other professors, in which our relationship was not as strong. However, I can reach out to them for anything, and I am sure they will help me.

I lost contact with most of the people I worked with. If your needs are met elsewhere, why search out there for anything else. For the most part, work experience during high school and college is just that, experience to prepare you for your future opportunities.

Acquaintances

You have friends and you have acquaintances. Please keep them separate. Acquaintances are people you know, but you have not bonded with long enough to share a close friendship.

People have blurred the lines of friendship and an acquaintance, which causes problems down the line. No, you do not have to go around defining people, "you are my acquaintance and you are my friend."

It is not elementary school. I think you should keep lines drawn in the sand; you should not be sharing your deepest secrets with people you just met yesterday. Keep lines drawn but you can be vulnerable and honest with others.

You can share information, network, hangout, and communicate in some way. But when you are having problems in your relationships, or just broke up with your boyfriend, call your real friends, the ones you trust. The friend that will give you honest solid advice on what to do.

Now it is likely an acquaintance could give you the direction you need. It is also likely your information is not as safe in the hands of friends. Likewise, you never know when you cross paths with someone God wanted to be your friend. Keep an open mind when building friendships, you do not always have to hold back.

An acquaintance is someone you can network with or go to for advice. Do not purposely shut people out, or use them for your benefit, when you have no intentions on ever involving them in your life.

That is mean and offensive. I have people in my life who are acquaintances-- I never acknowledge them as such. I hang out with them, we have playdates with our kids, we talk on the phone, we Facebook, we have fun.

My relationships with my friends are completely different. I can talk on the phone with them for hours, we hardly every Facebook each other. We facetime/hangout, I travel to see them, we go on trips together, we pretty much communicate all the time.

Now I have some close friends who I only talk to sometimes, that is ok too, because when we do catch up, it is for hours.

I honestly hang out with my acquaintances more than I do my friends, because we may share the same interest and/or our schedules are similar, allowing more time to hang.

As you get older some of your close friends may become distant, and some of your acquaintances may end up being one of your best friends.

It takes time for relationships to build, my best advice is, get to know people, understand them, make time for them, and enjoy their company.

If they are good people, who are not bringing any drama into your life, they have never shown you any hatred, jealously, or are not a negative person --hey why not be friends. Learn to evaluate your friends along the way.

Enemies

Our enemies need love too. We owe them the most, because they are the ones that set us up for greatness. They are the ones who push us to work harder. They are the ones who prepare you for battle and to help you overcome obstacles.

They are the ones who bring you closer to God. Do not always look at it as a bad thing. Enemies bring good to life; they bring out your best.

Submission and Authority

Have you ever heard the saying, 'you are who you hang around?'

≈≈≈≈≈≈

1 Corinthians 15:33, (KJV).

[33] *Do not be misled: "Bad company corrupts good character."*[b]

≈≈≈≈≈≈

If you hang around people who do bad things, I am sure you will be tempted to do the same. If you hang around people who do good, have goals, dreams, and aspirations, you would do the same.

You cannot let all the things you go through in life stop you from becoming the person God has planned for you.

No matter the situation, we were all created with a purpose. The things we experience in life strengthens us. Your daily struggles are setting you up for tomorrows promises.

Tomorrow is not promised, but you also are expected to give your best every day. Giving your best today will set your standards and will count for tomorrows rewards.

Tomorrow is not promised, but who said tomorrow is not coming? It is coming.

Get Ready, Let Go, Let God, And Let's Grow!

We all need a village who has our best interest. Who's in your village? Who pulls the best out of you? Who keeps you accountable?

We all need a village who has our best interest. Who's in your village? Who pulls the best out of you? Who keeps you accountable?

_____
_____
_____
_____
_____
_____
_____
_____
_____
_____
_____
_____
_____
_____
_____
_____
_____
_____
_____
_____
_____
_____
_____
_____
_____
_____

Love

An intense feeling of deep affection.

The Tool of Love

Love is mentioned in the bible 131 times, according to www.christianbiblerefereces.org. Love should be without conditions, without limits, and without cause.

To love without condition means to love no matter what happens. No matter the offense by your neighbor, friend, sister, brother, or cousin. No matter your life situation, abandonment or parentless.

No matter if someone simply steps on your toes. To love a person at their worst and at their best at any given moment. To love a person as much as you love yourself.

Loving Yourself First

To understand what love truly means and to be able to give and show love to others, you have to be able to love yourself. Love yourself for who God created you to be.

You are beautiful and created perfectly. I want you to get to a place where you love everything about yourself, the good and the ugly.

Yes, I said ugly, because some of you think the worst about yourself.

Maybe your forehead is too large or nose too wide. I have heard some of the most ridiculous things. It is not true. Your forehead is the size God wanted it to be. Your nose is the size it is supposed to be.

I used to hate being tall. I stand five feet nine. Most of my friends are under five foot five, I use to hate it. Now I have learned to embrace it. God created me to be a big boned tall woman for a reason.

Instead of tearing yourself down, build yourself up. If someone says something about you that you do not agree with, so what. People are going to continue to talk and continue to downgrade others.

If we honestly lived by what others thought or said, we would not amount to anything in life. Love the things about yourself that you want to change. Love all your flaws and characteristic. Love yourself from head to toe, from inside and out.

I think we are our hardest critics. We do not need disapproval from others because we already think it about ourselves.

To love yourself means to know who you are, and who you belong to. You are a child of God. You belong to the most high.

You are worthy of all things. Yes, I mean all things. To love yourself is to have confidence, respect, and dignity. Before you can expect anyone to love you, you have to love yourself.

How can you give anyone positive energy, when you are down and cannot pick yourself up? How can you encourage anyone else if you cannot encourage yourself?

People are going to disappoint you, hurt your feelings and walk away. It is going to happen. People will mistreat you and abuse you. It is going to happen. People will devalue you, if you allow them.

Take control. You do not have control of how your life is planned. You do have control of how you react to people, and the things you accept from them.

Tools for Your Journey

You have every right to tell people how you deserve to be loved. Do not expect everyone to agree—everyone is not going to agree. These are the people that will walk away from you and dismiss you as though you are the problem.

Most likely you are not the problem, they probably have failed to love themselves, and now do not know how to give love to anyone else.

Through adversity you have to learn to love and accept yourself and everyone else for who they are. People are not perfect and you have to learn to love them, their imperfections, and support them along the journey.

See the best in everyone, even when they show you their worst. You determine your best and set the same standards for how people should love and care for you.

To love yourself is to know your worth. To know your worth is understanding your value in life and what you deserve in life. You have a choice to accept or refuse the cards you were dealt, as you get older and mature.

No, we cannot choose the families that God created for us, but we can choose who stays and goes.

We can choose our friends. There are cards dealt to us and cards we deal to ourselves.

It is not so much about the cards you have in your hand (life), it is about what you do with those cards.

I cannot compare life to the game of UNO or Spades, but I can use the analogy: you either sit and cry that you are losing or play those cards to the best of your ability.

Life requires you to do your best and learn as much as you can along the way.

No, we cannot all yell "UNO!" at the same time, but we can continue to play repeatedly, until you do WIN or accept that you have done your best.

I told my seven-year-old, do your best, that is all you can give. She always asks, "How do I know when it is my best?"

I explained to her that you know it is your best when you have given it your "all."

When you have pushed through without complaining or giving up. If your feel like your best is not enough, evaluate it, then try again.

It is true, we are not going to always win, we are not going to always lose. Our wins provide experience. Our wins reflect our strength and courage.

Our losses, mishaps, and drops reflect our efforts. It shows you tried, you gave your best, you did not give up and you conquered. Conquering may not always be a win.

My goal is to always give my best. That is my standard. I am always a winner in my book. Why, because I took something away from the experience, I got it done, and enjoyed it.

Keep your head up when you are in a situation and going downhill. Determine what was missing during your downhill spiral and work towards collecting those tools to get to where your trying to go.

> There is an uphill for every downhill, and a downhill for every uphill.
> Turkish Proverb

Let's go over some things you "physically" need going up-hill.

We must start with hiking boots. Have you ever tried hiking in gym shoes or rain boots? Ha, it is no fun.

Allow my experience to lead you in the right direction. You need water, it is exhausting going uphill. You must stay hydrated. You are going to need a first aid kit, who knows, you may fall along the way- we all fall short sometimes, especially if your endurance is not up to speed.

Going uphill in life you are going to need tools and resources that will help you on your journey.

You cannot complete this journey without help. You cannot do it on your own. Imagine your journey without direction, tools, and resources — we would be completely lost.

Try traveling to a new place without GPS or google maps, how far do you think you would get?

How would you know where to begin or which way to go? It would be difficult and probably frustrating trying to get to your destination. Same with life – it does not have to be that way though.

Yes, we must endure trials and tribulations, but who said you could not have help along the way.

Life is not meant to be traveled alone. We cross paths with people, on our journey, intentionally by God. It is true --people are around for a reason, season, and life time.

We have to learn to accept it, learn from it, and continue to move on in life. People are here to make us better and we are around others to make them better.

I do not understand it when people say, "I'm not a people person." Without being a people person, you will never grow or prosper.

People are around to give us what we need and vice versa. Think about all the people who have taught your life lessons, or people who have given you a tool to use that you still use today.

If we had never crossed their paths, we would not be the person we are today. We learn so much about ourselves, being connected to people.

Another way you can start is by using the twelve tools I've provided in this book. These are the tools I use to help define my successes (wins), health, and leadership goals.

Do not allow people, to define the way you should be loved or your value. If you allow people to love you the way they want to love you, and define your value, you are allowing others to determine your worth and your greatness.

Everything God created is "Good." As you read Genesis, he said, "everything was created out of goodness." So, if He created everything to be good, what is wrong with how He created you?

People walk around hard on the inside, as if they do not need love. They act like they do not need anyone or any help. They act as if they have it all going on, and all their ducks are in order.

Before judging someone, you have to understand their situation. To understand their situation, you have to get to know that person.

No, we are not going to get to know everyone we encounter on a personal level. Nonetheless, we have to see pass their situations, have compassion and empathy for others. Love others the way you would want to be loved.

Your ability to have empathy with their situation helps you to understand their intent. Begin to love people the way they deserve to be loved. Everyone deserves grace and mercy. Grace and mercy begins with love.

Unconditional Love

I am not going to say it is easy to love without conditions. I struggled through my life during my twenties to love unconditionally. However, at the age of twenty-eight, I had begun to understand how to create safe boundaries, while learning to love unconditionally, and loving others from a distance.

Before learning how to love, I sought revenge and let a lot of people go out of my life. If they did not love me the way I expected to be loved or what I thought love was, they got the boot.

Now, when I look back on my life, I would have taken back some things I said that hurt others, and some people I have cut out of my life.

I do not live a life of regrets; however, I do seek to find a take away from each lesson. I miss a lot of those individuals genuinely, and if friendships are meant to be repaired, it will surely happen.

Loving unconditionally is not only towards your family, children, or friends. God expects us to love all people as if they were family. God calls us to be servants to his people. We are expected to take care of one another and make sure everyone is well.

Loving without limits does not mean settling for less and accepting any kind of disrespect or abuse (physical or mental). Learning to love, at a distance, is not a terrible thing. This process is needed for situations when you love someone so much, but cannot stand to be around them, because of the things they have done to you or others.

When you love someone at a distance, you keep in touch and spend time with them on your terms.

I feel as though this process is also needed, when you allow that person to grow and mature in particular areas. You see their potential, through the storm, and wait out the time for them to progress and bloom.

This process is called, "being long suffering with people." A good friend, once taught me a true lesson, about being long suffering with my family.

Sometimes, family is hard to love, but they were created by God and it is absolutely nothing you can do about it. As stated before, family is an appropriate use for boundaries. Learning to love people during their storm and being there for them when they come out is true love.

The question we should ask one another is; "If people do not know how to love themselves, how can they love other people?"

If people cannot see the best in themselves, how can they give someone else their best. This goes for all relationships. To love yourself, first, you have to understand the love God has for you.

Just know, no matter what you go through or how you feel, God will always love you. He will always be there for you. Just as He is there for you, you have to be there for him.

Changing Lives Through My Testimony

Have faith and know your current situation is not your final destination. I have been in a place where I could not see any hope.

I questioned my existence with God. I questioned my life with God. I even blamed him, a few times, for certain situations in my life. It happens, we are not perfect.

Things happen. Life is not perfect. Your mother or father may have abandoned you.

Your friends may not have been there when you needed them the most. Your siblings may have failed you.

Your teachers may have said, "you will not amount to anything in life."

Tools for Your Journey

Just know as you need help with your situation, they needed help too. Maybe they did not know how to ask for help. Maybe they did not know how to love you, like you deserved to be loved.

Maybe they did not receive the love they deserved as a child. We can either speak life, in our situation, or we can speak death. We can look at all the things we go through, that keep us down, and continue to entertain it; or we can begin to use them as stepping stones, to get to the top by speaking life (good things).

We can choose to ask for healing, to stop the generational curses in our families, or we can choose to continue with them. Life does not come with Band-Aids, we cannot keep patching up losses and mistakes.

It is noteworthy to get to a place where you are your biggest supporter and cheerleader. Always look for gratification from within yourself.

If we continue to look for others to push us to the next level, we will not make it to the top. To get to the top, it takes, determination, motivation, and self-will. It takes you believing, "I got this and I am going to conquer."

The "top" is defined by you. You cannot allow others to dictate or determine your expected success.

Goal setting is a lifestyle and only the people determined to succeed will accomplish each goal set forth.

No matter what, continue to love yourself first and share the love with everyone else around you. Love people the way you would like to be loved.

The cure for hate in this world is love, and there is so much to go around.

What does love mean to you?

Tools for Your Journey

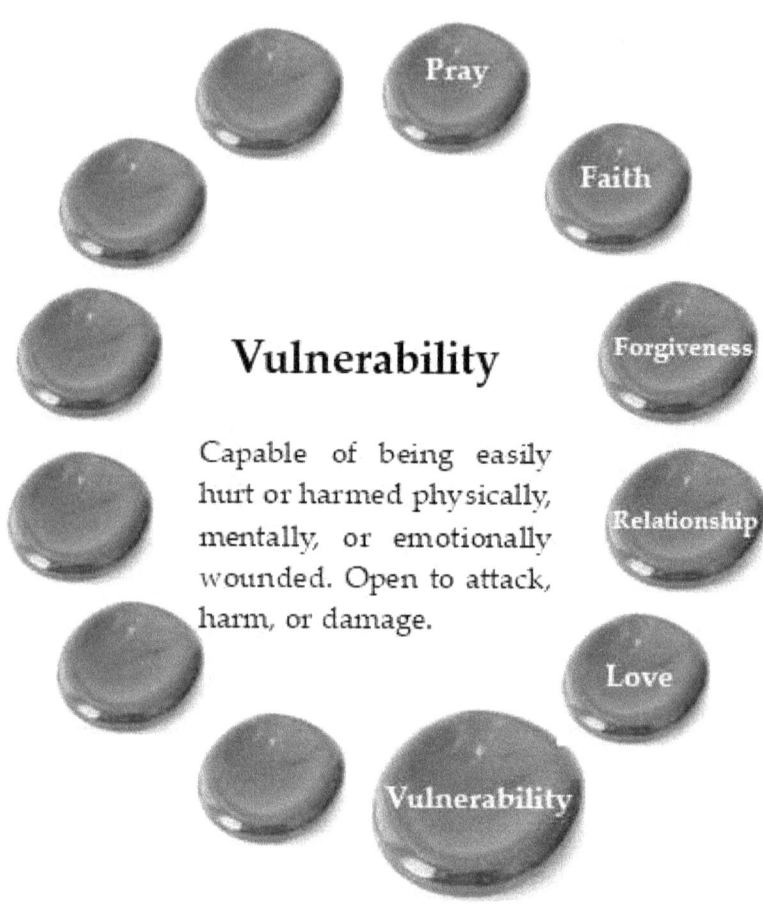

The Tool of Vulnerability

To be vulnerable is to be open and honest with yourself first. Being completely confident with communicating your emotions. Not being overly emotional or wearing your emotions on your sleeve, but knowing what to say and when to say it.

It is okay to express your feelings, but you do not have to say everything. Some things are better unsaid.

When you are honest with yourself, you can be honest and open with other people connected to you. We are placed on earth to connect with people; whether family, friends, co-workers, teachers, neighbors, etc. We were placed here to be a service to other's and take care of one of another.

Vulnerability has been looked upon in a negative light; being easily hurt, succumb to temptation, unacceptable to criticism, pressure, defensive, or distressfully exposed.

Vulnerability is accepting criticism, direction and still being able to push through. We are all human, we all have experienced a time in our lives when our feelings have been hurt.

There is nothing wrong with showing your emotions and allowing people to see and feel your hurt. There is nothing wrong with expressing your feelings in a positive way, and letting others know how you feel.

You have to be transparent with people, especially those you are trying to help, or make a difference in their lives.

At the age of 29, I felt like I was overly emotional. I cried a lot more than I ever had before in my late twenties. Before, I always appeared to have it together all the time.

People use to be intimidated by me. They thought I was arrogant and had an air about myself.

When I did have my moments, when I openly expressed my emotions, they looked at me as if I was crazy — like I was tripping.

It was not because I was perfect. It was because I never showed my struggles. I hid them well. I was not the type of person who would ask for help when I needed it the most.

I guess I had a sense of pride about myself. I figured I was in control of my life, and I made sure I did not need help from anyone.

I carried that attitude into adulthood. It is perceived as if you have it together all the time, you do not need anything from anyone, and you know it all. What are people going to think of you? What are they going to think of themselves? No, we cannot control other people's insecurities, but we can do something about the way we offend others.

When you are vulnerable your heart is softer. You have more compassion and love for people. Imagine walking around holding everything inside. For instance, your hurt from childhood to adulthood.

Once you become an adult, how do you think you will feel and how do you think you would react to people, especially those who have hurt you or continue to hurt you?

Vulnerability is not a sign of weakness; it is a sign of strength. I used to believe asking for help makes you a weak person. I wanted to always get it done by myself.

My mother instilled a mentality that no one wants to help you. Since I thought no one wanted to help me, I learned to get it done always by myself, not even with my mother's help.

I never asked anyone for help. I worked sun up to sun down, by making sure Sears marketing and advertisements were displayed correctly; making sure orders at McDonalds, Wendy's and dining services in the student union were filled.

I believed in working for whatever I needed and wanted. I made sure I kept a job.

We are not perfect and things are going to happen. It is not what happens or how it happens, it is what we do after it happens that matters.

As young women, we must learn to be real with ourselves. Be honest with ourselves. The problem in most relationships is that people are not true to themselves.

People are busy trying to be something they are not and putting on an act for people in their lives. Problems in relationships are much deeper than the surface situations.

You have to learn how to balance your life. Allow people to help you along the way. You will not be able to do it all by yourself. Life just does not work out that way.

You have to be open to being hurt. Learn to let your guard down. When we are at our lowest point in life is when most of us call out to God. That is when we learn our biggest lessons and mature into the person we were created to be. We grow from our weaknesses.

We all have them. Yes, we will wrestle with our old nature. I do not think anyone likes changes; however, change is needed for prosperity. Change is needed for growth.

Strive to get to a place where you can acknowledge things you have done wrong, apologize if you need to and move on. You cannot beat yourself up because you missed the mark or consider yourself a failure. You must learn to admit your wrongs and find a way to continue with life.

Bonus Tool of Resilience

Resilient

: able to become strong, healthy, or successful again after something bad happens

I am going to restate this continuously; things will happen to good people and things happen to us all. It is not what we do when they happen, it is how you handle picking up the pieces and continuing to move forward.

Being resilient is all about how you handle the situation after it has happened. You cannot allow anything to hold you back. You have to be consistent in your ability to bounce back because things will happen all the time.

What will you do? Are you going cry in a corner or rise to the occasion and conquer it like a champ?

A wise person told me, "You only get two seconds to have your temper tantrum, when your upset about something; after your seconds are up, it is time to figure out what to do next."

What are you going to do to fix the problem? What are your plans? Now it is time to implement. It is time to do the work. You have been given six tools already. Come on let's move on to the *Tool of Confidence*.

Tools for Your Journey

Your Notes for the Day

The Tool of Confidence

What does being confident mean to you? Is confidence earned, provided, or given to us? Are we taught how to be confident. Do we wait until others define our confidence? Do we wait until others boost our confidence?

Think about it - if you wait around for others to define your worth or value, you will be waiting forever. It is possible, people will devalue you, bring your confidence down, and label you as something you are not.

Confidence is not something that naturally happens. Confidence is something you obtain internally. Some people confuse confidence with self-esteem.

Confidence is how you define your ability to do certain things.

Self-esteem is a measure of the way you value yourself; self-respect.

To have self-esteem is to know who you are; know your worth; love yourself with all your flaws and baggage. To be confident is to have enough assurance to do whatever it takes to accomplish your goals and get the job done.

I say flaws and baggage, because we all have things about ourselves we want to change. We have things about ourselves we dislike and carry with us.

We all have them. But it is okay, there is always room for self-reflection and growth. Being confident comes with work each day. We live and learn from our experiences. Growth should take place each day.

We have to get to a place, where we are not worried about every little thing someone says about us. You are beautiful, just the way you are, and life is going to be okay.

We have to learn to walk with our heads held high. People are not always going to be there to push you along the way. You have to learn how to encourage yourself, motivate yourself and get the job done. Who or what are you waiting for?

We cannot always wait around for the next person to say, "job well done," with a pat on the back.

Learn to pat yourself on the back. Learn to reward yourself, when you feel you have done something worth celebrating.

Your wins are your wins- not anyone else's. One remarkable thing about our wins, is that it still gives others hope. You cannot always wait around for the crowd to applaud you. Learn to be happy for yourself.

There will be times when we receive standing ovations and there are times when we will not. At the end of the day, know that glory goes to God. He is happy for you and proud to call you his child. Having faith in God and believing everything will be okay, is what has gotten me this far in life and that is all you and I need.

I cannot say I have always been a confident person. I can say I have always stood out in a crowd. I am very different from a lot of young women I grew up with.

Different, meaning I felt outcast and did not belong. Even as young women mature, they are still cliquish. I was not the kid that ran with a group or clique. I did not fit in with any group of kids.

I did not talk like most kids my age. I did not look like them nor did I act like them.

As any typical kid, I tried to do things, as others did, to fit in. I tried most things young kids tried. I tried being the rebellious kid, who got sent to the principal's office. I tried being the kid who always disobeyed their teachers.

I tried fighting, changing my language by cursing and using very ugly words. Seeking negative attention, will always get you negative consequences and results.

When I went to college I worked three jobs to keep up with other people. Yes, I tried to keep up with the Joneses. I shopped at Victoria Secret wearing PINK and I made sure I had the latest Jordan's. I went out to the clubs and attempted to go to every college party.

As I got older, I realized I never enjoyed any of it. I never enjoyed working all those hours, hanging out to the early hours of the morning, or being sprayed by pepper spray from police officers, trying to man the crowds of young adults fighting over disagreements.

I was not the popular one, nor was I the person that had multiple cliques of friends. Through elementary, middle, high school and college, I have never followed the crowd. Although I was not a follower, I wanted to know why I was so different. Although I tried to fit in, it never worked. I was never one of them.

Today I understand why God set me aside from everybody else. He set me aside and isolated me, to elevate me and define the greatness he had planted in me.

He could not work on me, while I was trying to fit in, and doing things I knew I should not have been. Reflecting on my life experiences, transitioning from adolescent to young adulthood, I now understand my journey, my boldness, and confidence.

I had to go through those things, so I could make a difference in others' lives. Now that I have been where you may be today, I am able to help you, get to a place you want to be within yourself.

Confidence comes from within. You obtain it internally. Nobody is handing out free confidence. You cannot purchase it. You cannot make it. You cannot steal someone else's confidence.

Confidence is a state of mind, it is how you think about things and how you process your way of life.

Confidence takes work. You have to constantly train your mind to think positive. There are many ways to boost your confidence. First, you can start by having a conversation with yourself.

Look at yourself in the mirror and say, "I am what I say I am. I am beautiful, smart, wise, intelligent, a leader, and the change I want to see in the world. I am a person of integrity, grace and class."

If you are, stop being so hard on yourself. Stop worrying about what others think of you. If you are doing your best and seeking opportunities for growth, why does it matter. If you are not walking around intentionally hurting people, causing problems, or putting others down, why does it matter what other people think?

If someone says something bad about you, and cannot give you positive advice to self-evaluate or work towards, why are you entertaining what they are saying?

People, who are not bringing any good to your life, and you are not able to effectively bring good in their life, move on from them. Some people are just negative people. Their help comes from the Lord and you just have to pray for them.

It is difficult maturing when so many people are against you. Few people will look like you, talk like you, or act like you.

I have always been that kid who made awesome grades, did what I was told and always participated in school extracurricular activities.

On the other hand, you have others around you, that make decisions, to do their own thing and go against rules and make bad choices. We have all been told not to follow the crowd. Stop doing what others are doing and stop doing things to fit in, it is not adding value to your life.

On most occasions, you are the one suffering the consequences. When you are reaping the consequences, the crowd you were following, will disappear without warning.

Confidence Boosters
- Try reconditioning the way you think about your life.
- Know your strengths and weaknesses.
- Accept your mistakes and flaws.
- Accept compliments and compliment yourself.
- Use criticism as a learning experience.
- Try to stay joyful, cheerful and have a positive outlook on life.

What I love about myself ....

Tools for Your Journey

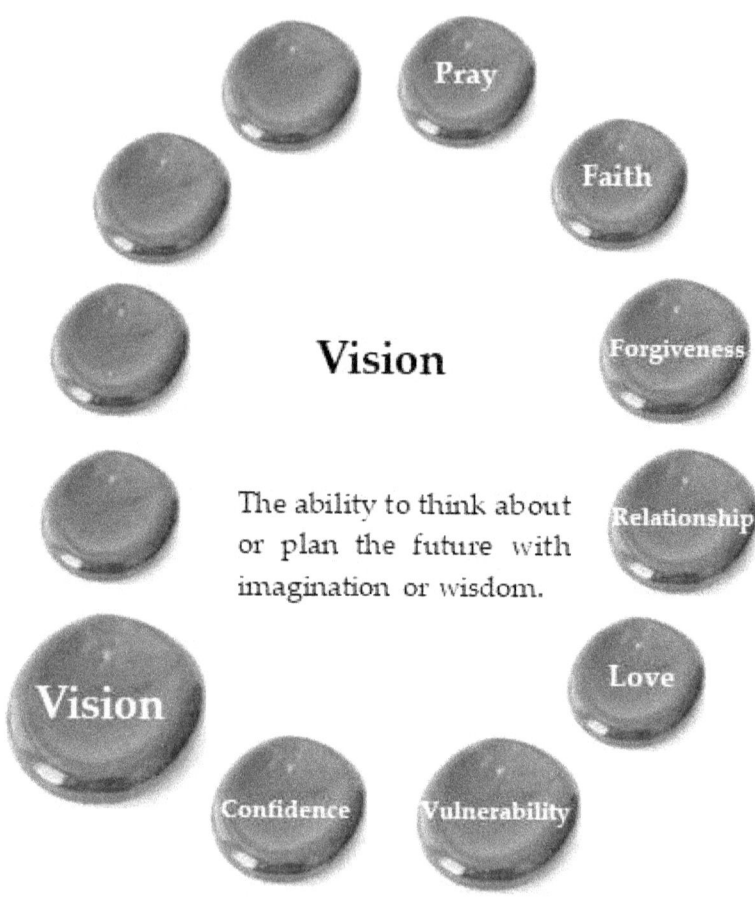

Tool of Vision

≈≈≈≈≈≈

Proverbs 29:18, (KJV).
18 Where there is *no vision, the people perish: but he that keepeth the law, happy* is *he.*

≈≈≈≈≈≈

I have always had dreams and visions, of being well known and successful. I always felt I had the talent to walk in the biggest runway fashion shows, attend events with other well-known people, receive awards for my work in the community, sit on Oprah's stage being interviewed and sharing my story and journey with the world.

This portrayal could take on a selfish or prideful picture, as if someone owes me something. I learned early in life to work hard for what I wanted.

It is not so much that I care about the lavish life and the glam. This picture I created was a vision of what success looks like in my eyes.

Material things do not define success, its defined by your life experiences. Material things comes and go, but no one can take away the experiences you had along your journey.

≈≈≈≈≈≈

Ecclesiastes 3:13 (KJV).

[13] *And also that every man should eat and drink, and enjoy the good of all his labour, it is the gift of God.*

≈≈≈≈≈≈

The hardest part about creating a vision, and developing a plan is implementing the plan. Working towards every desire of your heart. Do the research to obtain the resources you need for the journey to your next goal.

I can be a bit impatient at times, while working towards my goals. A major struggle for me is procrastination. I am sure I have a few witnesses that can join me to say, "I am a procrastinator."

I do so many things at the last minute. Many define procrastination as a negative characteristic, but it depends on the situation. Procrastination brings out my best work. I love working under pressure.

Without growth, there is no change and without change there is no growth. Consider starting this journey to success and be open to change.

What Is Your Purpose?

What is my purpose? We were all called (created) to do something. Our job is to figure out what God has called us to do. We were placed on earth, to be of service to others in one or many ways. There are people, who believe, we were called to do many things. There are others, who believe, we are only called to do one thing.

If we were called to do one thing, why do we have a passion to do many things. Passion has many meanings. The translation I want to reference: passion being an intense desire or enthusiasm for something.

Now that can mean anything. I once heard, "If you cannot figure out your purpose, figure out your passion."

Your passion will lead you right into your purpose. Whenever I am helping young women with goals and planning, I ask, "What are you passionate about?" Many do not know.

No matter how many times I have heard "I do not know," each time it drives me bananas.

How is it that we were all created and called to do something, but many of us, do not know what that something is?

Many individuals do not know what they are passionate about. Think about what makes your heart happy? There are many things I am passionate about. Writing is one of them.

Through writing, I think people obtain more information than listening to me speak. I love expressing myself through writing. I believe if people take time to read and write more they will obtain more information. They will relate to the words more and gain a better understanding of what is being said.

When you are speaking, people do not always know how to actively listen. I am a witness. While someone is telling you something, you are already preparing a whole speech in your head, ready to respond and sometimes miss the entire conversation because you were not listening.

Actively listening is being 100% engaged in the conversation. Listen to the other persons entire spiel, before analyzing and responding.

Our purpose is defined: as a reason in which something is done or created or for which something exists. Wow, now we all were created for a reason, with purpose.

If you pray about it, God will answer you. He will order your steps and direct your path.

≈≈≈≈≈≈≈

Exodus 9:16, (KJV).
16 And in very deed for this cause *have I raised thee up, for to shew* in *thee my power; and that my name may be declared throughout all the earth.*

≈≈≈≈≈≈≈

God created you with purpose, he has given you his power, that he may have full glory for your destiny. You were created out of greatness. God's spirit lives through you when you believe.

Second Guessing

Go with your first mind when you have a gut feeling about something positive. We hurt ourselves when we go back and forth with a decision.

We are double minded. Women have the gift of gut feelings (intuition). Learn how to use your power effectively and go with your first mind. Your gut is telling you, noooo – do not do it or yes do it. Your gut is the holy spirit guiding you in the right direction, learn to listen and move with God's help.

Greatness in You And I

God has destined greatness for each of us. When I think about the times, I felt unworthy of his blessings, I was reminded about the time Jesus died for us, so our lives would be saved.

The best reward (gift) we can earn is life, everlasting life. God has riches and wealth stored for each one of us. There is room for us all to make it to the top.

However, we fight with each other and become envious and jealous of other's blessings. But why?

There is room for everyone to make it and we should want everyone to make it. We should work just as hard for the next person to make it, as we worked for ourselves.

You will not be able to tap into the blessings God has for you, with a selfish or jealous heart and envious spirit. We will not receive God's rewards for us until we learn to love.

Your Notes for the Day

Tools for Your Journey

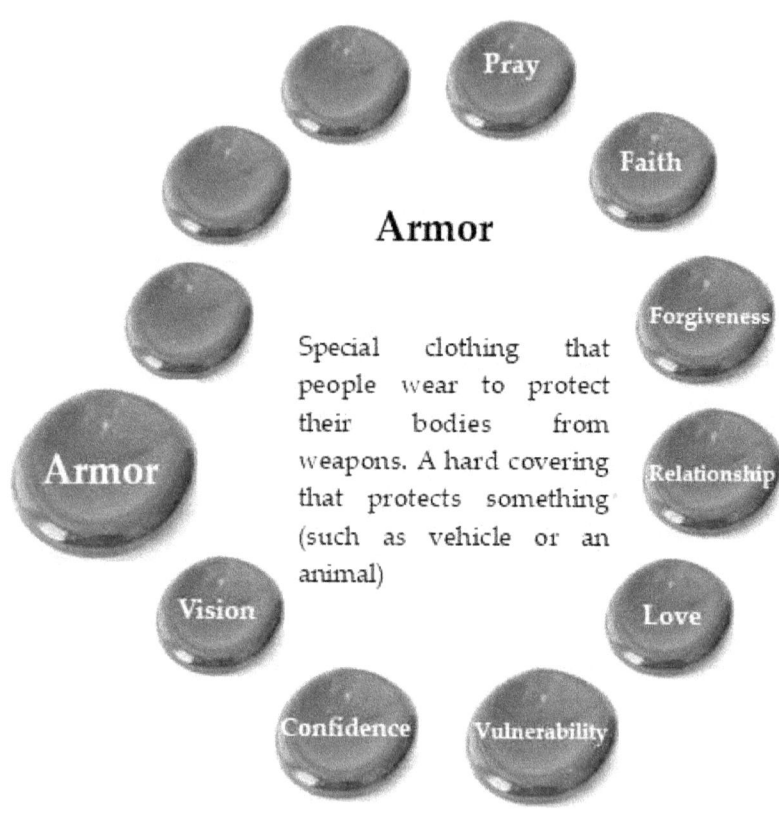

The Tool of Armor

When I think of armor, I think of our responsibility, to use the power that God gave us, to protect our vessels (mind, body, and spirit) from the enemy.

Be knowledgeable about your needs and wants. Be knowledgeable about things in life that make your heart happy, drives your passion, and gets you to your end goal.

During war, our soldiers use armor to protect themselves from their enemies. To go further in history, our soldiers previously used brass shields (brass armor) to protect themselves from arrows, bullets, or whatever else other armed forces sent their way.

God provides us the same protection daily, an armor to use in the same manner as our soldiers during war. It is spiritual. Let's run through the "whole armor" of God:

The Whole Armor of God

≈≈≈≈≈≈

Ephesians 6:10-20, (KJV).

[10] *Finally, my brethren, be strong in the Lord, and in the power of his might.*

[11] *Put on the whole armour of God, that ye may be able to stand against the wiles of the devil.*

[12] *For we wrestle not against flesh and blood, but against principalities, against powers, against the rulers of the darkness of this world, against spiritual wickedness in high [places].*

[13] *Wherefore take unto you the whole armour of God, that ye may be able to withstand in the evil day, and having done all, to stand.*

[14] *Stand therefore, having your loins girt about with truth, and having on the breastplate of righteousness;*

[15] *And your feet shod with the preparation of the gospel of peace;*

[16] *Above all, taking the shield of faith, wherewith ye shall be able to quench all the fiery darts of the wicked.*

[17] *And take the helmet of salvation, and the sword of the Spirit, which is the word of God:*

[18] *Praying always with all prayer and supplication in the Spirit, and watching thereunto with all perseverance and supplication for all saints;*

[19] *And for me, that utterance may be given unto me, that I may open my mouth boldly, to make known the mystery of the gospel,*

[20] *For which I am an ambassador in bonds: that therein I may speak boldly, as I ought to speak.*

≈≈≈≈≈≈

It does not say, put on half of the whole armor, or three-fourths of the armor. It clearly tells us to put on the whole-- the entire armor of God, so we will be prepared for what the world has to offer.

Just because they offer us things, does not mean we should accept, acknowledge, or respond.

≈≈≈≈≈≈≈

Ephesians 6:12, (KJV).
12 For we wrestle not against flesh and blood, but against principalities, against powers, against the rulers of the darkness of this world, against spiritual wickedness in high [places].

≈≈≈≈≈≈≈

We are not fighting against the flesh. It is not the person you see, it is what lives inside of them. We are fighting with Satan and his nation of people.

Satan comes ready and prepared each day. Yes, he stays on ready. Why is it we are not ready, for what he has to offer us?

We are always ready to give him what he wants, aggressiveness, violence, and anger. We are not even ready for the small petty things we respond to daily. We allow for the smallest offenses to affect our entire day. I am not perfect, I am a witness to it also. But since I know better, I have to do better.

≈≈≈≈≈≈≈

Ephesians 6:13, (KJV).
13 Wherefore take unto you the whole armour of God, that ye may be able to withstand in the evil day, and having done all, to stand.

≈≈≈≈≈≈≈

God provided us enough power to take a stand during war. You do not have to physically hurt anyone. You do not have to use our "hands" to get back at anyone.

You also do not have to argue with people. You do not have to entertain their shenanigans or craziness. All you have to do is stand still. Believe me you will get through it and survive.

Stand still by keeping your cool. Walk away from fights and arguments, until people are ready to rationalize with you, like a normal person with effective communication.

Stand still by praying and giving it to God. This is when you open your mouth and use God's words to win each battle. The battle is not yours it is the Lord's.

Nonetheless, it is your job to pray to him and ask for help. Pray to him and ask for direction. He will provide.

≈≈≈≈≈≈≈

Ephesians 6:14-15, (KJV).

14 Stand therefore, having your loins girt about with truth, and having on the breastplate of righteousness;

15 And your feet shod with the preparation of the gospel of peace;

≈≈≈≈≈≈≈

You have to be ready to speak a word in all situations, especially during battle. Studying and meditating, on your readings, helps keep you ready with the word. Every day we should fill our spirits with the gospel, not only to help ourselves, but to help someone else in the time of need. How can you speak the word if you are not ready with a word?

Be ready so you do not have to get ready.

≈≈≈≈≈≈≈

1 Peter 5:8, (KJV).

8 Be sober, be vigilant; because your adversary the devil, as a roaring lion, walketh about, seeking whom he may devour:

≈≈≈≈≈≈≈

Imagine a lion walking around looking for its prey, the devil does the same thing. Watching and looking for someone to call his own. He's always recruiting without permission.

Being sober is being alert and attentive to what is going on around you. You have to pay attention to things happening in life. Stay in the word (constantly reading and meditating) and use it as your weapon as it was created to do. Your needs, wants, riches, protection, service – it is in the word. Tell God what he said he will do. In the mist of your situation pray.

≈≈≈≈≈≈

Ephesians 6:16, (KJV).

16 Above all, taking the shield of faith, wherewith ye shall be able to quench all the fiery darts of the wicked.

≈≈≈≈≈≈

Quench means to cool it down. Your shield of faith would protect anything hot (anything against you) coming your way; including the hate from our enemies or people who do not have your best interest.

Know that everyone is not against you. Pray for discernment to know the difference. Believe God, for what he said he would do. He keeps his word. If he said he will do it, He will. But it will all rest on your faith.

≈≈≈≈≈≈

Ephesians 6:17-18, (KJV).

17 And take the helmet of salvation, and the sword of the Spirit, which is the word of God:

18 Praying always with all prayer and supplication in the Spirit, and watching thereunto with all perseverance and supplication for all saints;

≈≈≈≈≈≈

Prayer is our life line to God. Prayer is how we communicate with God. Start your day with prayer, pray throughout the day and pray before you go to sleep at night.

"Helmet of Salvation," keep your eye on the prize, eternal life. There is so much that goes on in this world. We are not perfect, we will fall short, however, never disconnect from your heavenly father.

Never go too far left, where you are losing your direction in life. As we grow and mature, we will begin to learn more of who we are, and how our body reacts to certain things.

When we start seeing signs of our disconnection with God, such as: depression, loss of appetite, loneliness, etc.; figure out where those feelings are coming. Pray about it and seek help from your counsels, friends, teachers, advisors, family, and friends.

Focus your attention on God and his gift of salvation for us. He is a healer and protector, for all things, and guides us in the right direction.

≈≈≈≈≈≈≈

Hebrews 4:12, (KJV).

12 For the word of God is quick, and powerful, sharper than any two-edged sword, piercing even to the dividing asunder of soul and spirit, and the joints and marrow, and is discerner of the thoughts and intents of the heart.

Ephesians 6:19, (KJV).

19 And for me, that utterance may be given unto me, that I may open my mouth boldly, to make known the mystery of the gospel,

≈≈≈≈≈≈≈

What God does for us is a mystery. He knows all, but we do not know what blessings we are going to receive.

When wonderful things happen in our lives, or God answers a prayer unexpectedly, it is important to share our testimony, especially to nonbelievers.

I have experienced an abundance of prayers answered right on time. I did not know how it was going to happen, but I believed God would show up.

Sharing the mystery of the gospel is not about bragging about the things you have.

Please stay humble and always have a giving heart in the best interest of others. Share your stories, to help someone on their journey of faith.

An ambassador represents or promotes someone or something. An ambassador for Christ is a messenger.

≈≈≈≈≈≈

Ephesians 6:20, (KJV).
[20] *For which I am an ambassador in bonds: that therein I may speak boldly, as I ought to speak.*

Romans 13:11-14, (KJV).
[11] *And that, knowing the time, that now [it is] high time to awake out of sleep: for now [is] our salvation nearer than when we believed.*
[12] *The night is far spent, the day is at hand: let us therefore cast off the works of darkness, and let us put on the armour of light.*
[13] *Let us walk honestly, as in the day; not in rioting and drunkenness, not in chambering and wantonness, not in strife and envying.*
[14] *But put ye on the Lord Jesus Christ, and make not provision for the flesh, to [fulfil] the lusts [thereof].*

≈≈≈≈≈≈

We now understand and know about the armor of God. The armor has many pieces that work together as one. It is impossible to be effective, while only using part of the armor.

The breastplate is one of the key pieces of the armor. Without the breastplate, our entire soul would be exposed and unprotected. We would not be ready to fight our spiritual war with the world. Remember Satan stays on ready, so why not stay ready for him.

Your Notes for the Day

Tools for Your Journey

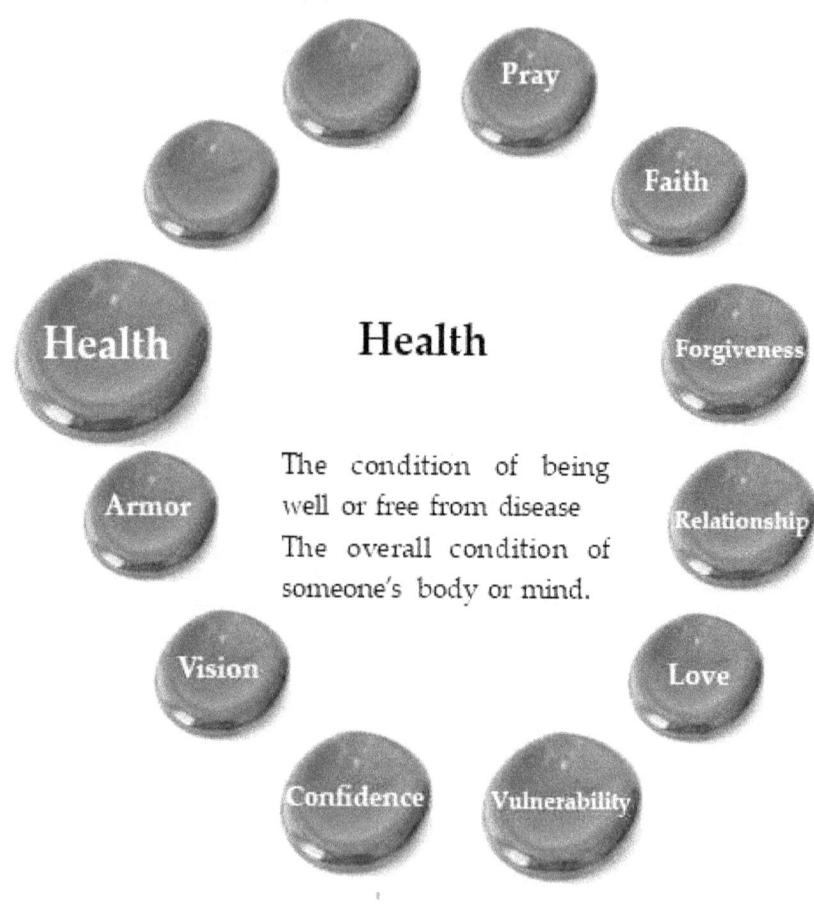

The Tool of Health/ Wellness

Overall health is essential to living a healthy life. Physical health begins with understanding your body and its needs. Everyone's body is different and desires different things.

I can agree, living the healthiest life possible, can be difficult and time consuming. Choosing to live a healthy life, is a "life style" not a movement or a trend. You have to work towards taking care of your body every day, all day.

We currently live, in times, where food prices rise and our foods are pumped with hormones, preservatives, and other things our body struggles to process.

Natural and organic foods do exist; however, they are overpriced. With a high demand, they are not going to drop the prices.

Have you noticed foods that are less healthy, are lower in price, and you get more food for your buck? These days, you can go to any fast food restaurant, and get an entire meal for five dollars. That is something to think about.

All unhealthy foods are reasonably priced. Most people would rather eat unhealthy and cheap, as opposed to healthy and expensive.

We can sit around and complain every day and do nothing about achieving our healthy living or weight loss goals. Or we can do something about working towards achieving our goal and gaining a better understanding of the things our bodies need.

I have always struggled with weight issues. During my adolescent years, I thought I was too fat, my bone structure was too large, stomach too flabby and the list goes on.

Little did I know I was perfect; my stomach was not flabby and my BMI (Body Mass Index; the percentage of fat in your body) of eighteen percent, meaning I was perfect for my height and age.

At twenty-nine years old, I stand five feet nine inches, weigh around 225 and BMI of 32%. I may not look obese but according to our health standards, I am extremely overweight.

I cannot blame the weight on baby weight any more. I think I was much smaller, after giving birth to my daughter, than I am now. I know what my problem is, and since I have identified the problem I need to do something about it.

As of today, I have been doing something about it. I set my goal weight at heath standards for my height. Since I am 5 feet 9 inches, with a larger bone structure, I should weigh in around 150 to 170.

I am not that far off from reaching my goal. Reflecting on my childhood and adolescent years I was in shape and had a great body structure.

Learn to love who you are and the body you are blessed with. If you feel as though you can lose a few pounds or more, you must do something about it. It is not going to happen overnight, but you will begin to see results.

Check out the chart on the following page to learn and understand where you fall. Also check out the websites, it breaks the chart down by small, medium, or large body frame, to calculate your current BMI. It is important to educate yourself and gain a better understanding of your body.

Tools for Your Journey

Since being overweight, I have developed so many minor illnesses, then I have ever experienced in my lifetime.

	Weight in Pounds													
	120	130	140	150	160	170	180	190	200	210	220	230	240	250
4'6"	29	31	34	36	39	41	43	46	48	51	53	56	58	60
4'8"	27	29	31	34	36	38	40	43	45	47	49	52	54	56
4'10"	25	27	29	31	34	36	38	40	42	44	46	48	50	52
5'0"	23	25	27	29	31	33	35	37	39	41	43	45	47	49
5'2"	22	24	26	27	29	31	33	35	37	38	40	42	44	46
5'4"	21	22	24	26	28	29	31	33	34	36	38	40	41	43
5'6"	19	21	23	24	26	27	29	31	32	34	36	37	39	40
5'8"	18	20	21	23	24	26	27	29	30	32	34	35	37	38
5'10"	17	19	20	22	23	24	26	27	29	30	32	33	35	36
6'0"	16	18	19	20	22	23	24	26	27	28	30	31	33	34
6'2"	15	17	18	19	21	22	23	24	26	27	28	30	31	32
6'4"	15	16	17	18	20	21	22	23	24	26	27	28	29	30
6'6"	14	15	16	17	19	20	21	22	23	24	25	27	28	29
6'8"	13	14	15	17	18	19	20	21	22	23	24	25	26	28

Height in Feet and Inches

Underweight Healthy Weight Overweight Obese

Resources: (http://www.healthchecksystems.com/heightweightchart.htm or http://www.calculator.net/ideal-weight-calculator.html

Let me remind you, very minor. I have developed bronchitis, had knee surgery due to a tear while working out, back problems, knee problems, skin infections; my eczema gets out of control and flares up, stress, allergy reactions externally and internally. I have been a complete mess.

After doing much research I have arrived at the conclusion that it is because I am …
- Overweight.
- Do not eat enough in a day (3-6 times a day… small meals).
- Do not drink enough water (64 oz. x 2).
- Not exercising as I use to in the past.
- My immune system is low.
- Iron Deficient.
- Slow Metabolism (I bet a turtle could beat it).
- Not getting 8 hours of sleep nightly.

Since I know these things cause problems in my body, why wait until I develop diabetes or high blood pressure. Why wait until my doctor prescribe medication to help control something in my body, that is supposed to happen naturally?

I know a lot of young people eat whatever they want. As you grow older, you have to start paying attention to what you are eating. There are so many things, in our foods today, we have no clue what we are eating.

Start small, but start educating yourself, about certain foods, your body should not consume.

There are preservatives, hormones and color dyes your bodies should not consume. Start looking at the labels and ingredients. Start reading books – There is a lot of research on healthy diets. You have to pick up a book or look up an article that has the information you need.

To build my immune system, lose weight, raise my metabolism, and live longer, I have to start eating healthy meals throughout the day, exercise at least thirty minutes, three times a week, eat more protein and take my vitamin's daily.

Vitamins, have been created, to supply our body with nutrients and minerals, we are not receiving from our meals throughout the day. I do not want to develop any major life illnesses or diseases. While I am receiving these signs "that I am not healthy," I have to do something about it. I have already started my journey to weight loss. I look forward to sharing my results, and weight loss advice in the future.

I know we all have our favorite foods, we over indulge. I have my favorites as well; I will not stop eating them. However, you have to learn to eat in moderation.

Learn to balance your meals throughout the day. I started meal prepping a few years ago. I am not a person that loves to cook, however, I believe in cooking with a purpose, cooking smart, and using my time in the kitchen effectively.

Meal prepping allows you to cook everything you need for the week in one day. It also allows you to make sure, you are eating three – five small meals throughout the day. We should feed our bodies food to use for energy every two – three hours.

For example

Breakfast 8 am	Snack 11 am	Lunch 1 pm	Snack 3 pm	Dinner 7 pm
Oatmeal Banana 1 slice of Toast	Cup of Grapes Or 1 apple	Chicken Salad Carrots	Cup of yogurt, string cheese, or ½ cup almonds	Chicken Breast, green beans, and brown rice

No, I do not believe in diets. Diets are set up to fail. Up until you started dieting, you use to feed your body, whatever you wanted.

You have to slowly begin taking away foods that are not healthy. Not completely though. If you completely take it away, you will crave it, and once you get your hands on whatever it is, you are going to overindulge again.

My chiropractor advised me to eat my favorite snack after dinner. This may be good advice for you, too. She told me she has a drum stick (ice cream cone) every day after dinner.

She also informed me, she does not eat anything sweet throughout the day. Then rewards herself every night after dinner. If you feel as though, you will not be successful with rewarding yourself every day, pick a week day to reward yourself.

Most week days for me are Friday evenings. I am not about to diet and I am not about that life. You do not have to give up your favorite foods to live a healthy life.

We should learn to eat things in moderation. Small qualities at a time. Believe me I know; however, I am about living healthy and living a long time. You do not have to give up anything.

You are not supposed to deprive yourself of things you like. We are supposed to eat in moderation. Instead of having the entire box of cakes, just eat one.

Instead of eating the entire roll of Oreo's just eat a serving sizing. Start looking at the serving size and start reading the labels. If it has more than 5 ingredients, do not eat it. If it has ingredients you cannot pronounce, do not eat it.

If the entire inside is filled with ingredients, please, stop and put it down. There are many other foods, we are eating, that are harmful for our bodies. No, we are not aware of it, because we failed to do our research.

We have to educate ourselves first, then educate people. We are God's vessels, we are a temple. To live in his purpose and spread the gospel and inspire others; we have to lead by example.

Yes, it is hard, yes, it is difficult, but who said it would be easy. We are God's chosen; we have to do his work. It will be a challenge attempting to serve in our purpose being unhealthy and overweight.

We have to get up and MOVE like Michelle Obama said. I made a promise to myself and the world, I would accomplish my goal, and share my story to inspire and help others.

The light bulb, in my head clicked, when I developed a bacterial infection of the hair follicles. It lasted a whole month and I was one miserable person.

It was constant itching, burning, and inflammation. My whole thigh had a fever; it was so hot due to the inflammation. I knew it was time to stop eating dairy, cut back on sweets, and start taking care of my body.

Mental Health

I am not a certified mental health specialist. I am speaking from my experience. I have managed caseloads, and worked at an all-girl group home, serving clients diagnosed with major mental health illnesses.

Let's start with a definition of mental health. Mental health is a physical disease that attacks the body. It is a disease of the brain that causes a chemical imbalance.

Some people are born with mental health diseases, and others are affected by their environment. Mental health is the leading cause of death in the United States.

When people are not mentally stable, it is hard for them to live productive lives. Why, because it is hard for people to see pass their current mental state. As individuals age, and never receive the help, they never learn how to cope with their illness. Strategies have to be implemented that will help them live productive lives.

Mental Health Facts

- 1 in five American adults experience a mental health issue.
- 1 in ten young people experience a period of major depression.
- 1 in 25 Americans live with a serious mental illness, such as schizophrenia, bipolar disorder, or major depression.
- Suicide is the tenth leading cause of death in the United States. It accounts for the loss of more than 41,000 American lives each year, more than double the number of lives lost to homicide.
- Biological, psychological, and social factors can be a root of half of all mental.
- Mental Health is a silent killer.

Mental health is serious and should be managed by a professional. Mental health is nothing to joke about or make mockery of others. People who suffer from mental illnesses, need your help, support, and encouragement.

Being diagnosed with a mental illness, does not mean your life is over and the world is going to end. However, it does mean you should take it seriously, and do the work to be able to live a manageable life. Manageable, meaning still being able to work, play, attend school, and enjoy life.

Learn the signs of people suffering with mental health issues. There are many people, who struggle daily, without seeking help from anyone. Learn the signs of your friends, and loved ones, struggling in silence and alone. Many people struggle in silence, because of the stigma attached to mental health:

- People think You are crazy.
- Friendship losses.
- Social rejection.

Some Signs of People Struggling:
- Depression
- Eating disorders
- Anxiety
- Sleep problems
- Isolation

To those, who are struggling in silence, with anything that is causing you to be unhappy, I know how difficult it can be to fight this thing alone. I have struggled in silence too.

I have been in your shoes, I have felt depressed, lonely, rejected, and questioned my existence. I am here to give you hope.

I am here to tell you – you can do it. Please seek out help. Call the National Suicide Prevention Lifeline: 1(800) 273-8255, available 24 hours every day. Seek out help from a professional.

Spiritual Health

Spiritual health is key to it all. Think of your spiritual health as a branch, and the branch being connected to the vine. What is a branch without a root that gives it life and nutrients.

Imagine a tree branch, laying on the side of the road away from the trunk of the tree (the vine). It will eventually wither away, dry up – it is dead. We are spiritually dead, when we are not connected to our source of life.

Being spiritually dead means being disconnected from God.

≈≈≈≈≈≈≈

John 15:1-2, (KJV).

¹ I am the true vine, and my Father is the husbandman.

² Every branch in me that beareth not fruit he taketh away: and every [branch] that beareth fruit, he purgeth it, that it may bring forth more fruit.

≈≈≈≈≈≈≈

It is impossible to be rooted in the word when you are disconnected.

When we are spiritually dead, we do things we know we should not do. We do not fast, pray, study, or serve people the way they should to be served.

Without spiritual connection, it would be hard for us to know who we are and where we come from. It would be hard for us to have any sense of direction.

Spiritually healthy is defined by your religious faith, beliefs, values, principles, and morals. The way we do things in life fall back on our spiritual health. Being able to love, have compassion for others, find joy and life's fulfillments, is determined by our spiritual health.

It is hard to find your purpose in life, when you are spiritually disconnected. Be spiritually connected with your inner self and your inner soul.

Physical, mental, and spiritual health all works together. When you are spiritually healthy, you are happier, less stressful, have more energy to exercise, hang out with family, find your purpose, and enjoy life.

You have to learn to be self-connected. When you are self-connected you have a better understanding of yourself. Whenever you feel disconnected, start evaluating your current state of mind.

Tools for Your Journey

I have not always been able to self-evaluate, but as I matured I learned more about myself. I have learned when to pray, when to chase after God, when to walk away from things or people, when to shut up and when to stand still and allow God to work on my behalf.

It will not come overnight. Physical, mental, and spiritual health all takes work. You must work at it every single day. We do not get a day off. Even relaxing is a part of taking time out for you. You have to take care of yourself in order to be of service to others.

Your Notes for the Day

Tools for Your Journey

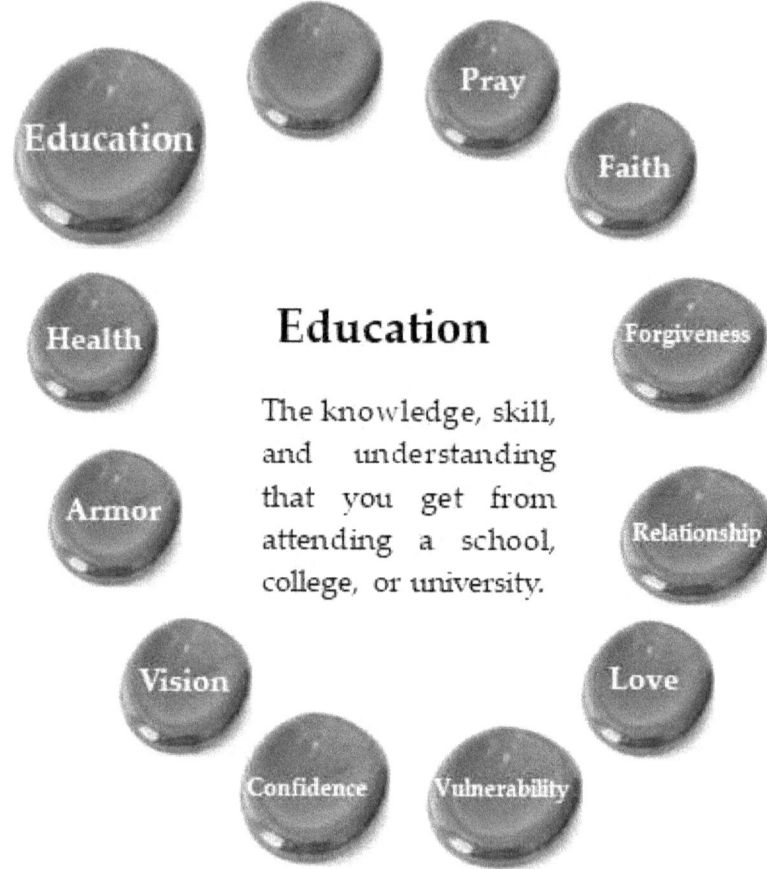

Education

The knowledge, skill, and understanding that you get from attending a school, college, or university.

The Tool of Education

"What do you want to be when you grow up?" – is the question we are asked as kids. Growing up, I knew I wanted to be a doctor and a lawyer. Some of us always knew what career field we were interested in; however, it is not always clear on how to get there.

You have to develop a plan, that helps your goals become clear to you. I knew I had to finish high school and go to college. But what happens between starting high school and graduating from college?

There is a lot that happens in between the years. Many of the youth today, do not think about the work that comes before the end of their high school years.

The years go by so fast. You will graduate from college and start your career in no time. I was not the kid who could not wait until I was grown.

I did not have to become an adult to know, I did not want that life too soon. Adults have bills and less money. I did not want that responsibility. I was in no rush to be a "grown up."

Reflecting on my college experience, I do not feel as though I put forth my best effort.

I was too involved in activities, and working too many part time jobs, to keep up with the 'Joneses.' I know you have heard the saying of "keeping up with the Joneses." Basically, trying to keep up with the same material things of others, you really cannot afford.

Education is a gift given to us many years ago. Yes, African Americans did not always have the same freedom of education as others. Today, in the United States, we are all offered a free education. We have to learn to take advantage, of what has been given to us and make the best of it.

We have to come to terms with our issues of the past. We cannot let our past experiences define who we are today.

We cannot let yesterday, define our tomorrow. We must use our experience, to motivate us to do better. To be better leaders for the next generation.

You do this by continuing to keep going. Keep trying. Yes, just keep swimming. Do not give up. In school, try your best. There is a difference, in doing your best falling short, compared to not giving your best and not trying at all.

There are many levels of schooling. Today, it is highly recommended to complete at least the first four to be successful and obtain a well-paying job. At one time, you could make thousands without a high school diploma. Today, you at least need a bachelor's degree to move up within a company.

Educational Goals:
1. Elementary
2. Middle School
3. High School Diploma or
   General Education Development Certificate
4. Associates and/or Bachelors
5. Masters
6. Ph.D. or Professional Degree

Towards the end of my last year of undergrad (academic education leading up to obtaining my Bachelor's Degree) I was informed that an associate's degree is compared to a high school diploma, a Bachelor degree is considered an associate, a Masters is considered a bachelor and a PhD is considered a Master's degree.

The value of each degree changes as the years go on. What does that mean? It means that a high school diploma is not enough anymore.

A bachelor's degree is a great asset, but not enough. I am encouraging you all, to at least obtain a bachelor's degree.

While in school, working towards your bachelors, I am encouraging you all, to complete an internship, to gain work experience. It will help you in the long run.

High School

High school is second to the most important years of school. You either make it or break it. Your GPA is important. Your participation in extracurricular activities are important. Your community service hours are important.

I would suggest college research early on in life. I suggest researching colleges, the first three years of high school. Why wait, until your senior year, to start researching for what you need to qualify for scholarships, both academic and athletic?

Believe me, there is someone already ahead of the game, before you thought about applying, in the fall quarter, of your last year of high school.

I am telling you this, because I was that student who missed college scholarships. My GPA was one point away from qualifying for a full ride scholarship.

I did not push myself to do better in my Senior year. I had average grades. Those average grades, were one point away from receiving a 4-year scholarship.

My tuition would have been paid in full. My only expense would have been room and board. Nope, I played games and missed out. Do not play around with your future college career.

The first day of your High School freshman year is the most important. Find out what sports or clubs your school offers. Find out what you want to put your time and energy into. Find other opportunities outside of your school.

Research organizations that offer scholarships. There are organizations such as Girl Scouts, Boys and Girls Club, and Urban League. They offer community service opportunities and career preparation, that would help you through your years of high school. Organizations for community service will prepare you for college and assist you with college tuition. Make those connections early and prepare throughout your high school years for your future career.

Get involved, there are also organizations that offer affordable college campus bus tours. They offer bus trips for college-bound high school students, that takes them across many states, to introduce them to multiple college campuses and college life all in one trip. It is a fantastic opportunity to get a taste of college life and receive curriculum information, entrance requirements, and financial resources.

College/Undergrad

It is a myth, you do not have to be certain of what you want to be when you grow up before stepping foot on a college campus. It is not a requirement, please do not allow that to deter you from enrolling into college. Once you step foot on a college campus the door opens to a world of opportunities.

You also do not have to enroll at a four-year college, starting out. Community colleges are just as good. It is important to get your electives out the way. Electives are college courses (classes) you choose to take that meets the humanities, language and arts, and science requirements for programs of your choice. However, many college students choose to attend a community college first, getting their electives out of the way, and saving thousands of dollars.

During your Freshman year in college, look into taking some introductory classes, for a major of your choice. Yes, there are many electives to choose from, however, there are also short cuts to taking electives.

You may take electives while in high school, over summer breaks, or electives that count twice for your major. Yes, double points.

Electives that count twice are courses required for your degree program and as a college elective.

Yes, you can use a course that fulfils an elective and course for your degree. Best thing ever implemented. Those are the best. If you have an awesome college advisor, you would already have known this little fact, if not, do not worry, now you do.

It is important to do your research, and do not rely solely on your academic counselor or advisors for choosing your classes. Choose wisely and enjoy your experience.

Most universities will not give you the secret to finishing on time, because they want you to be there longer to spend more money. Do your research and find the information necessary to complete your degree in a timely manner.

Your job, is to figure out your major and invest in your bachelors. You can complete a dual degree. Finishing with two bachelors or a bachelor and master's degrees.

While in high school, you can also graduate with an associate's degree and high school diploma. How cool would that be? You have a duty and your job is to be ahead of the game, not a step behind.

List of Schools your thinking about attending

School	GPA Required	Other requirements (personal statement, ACT score, etc.)

Student Loans

Student loans are funds borrowed from the federal government or private lenders, to pay for your college education. Let me whisper a secret - "student loans are not an option, for any of you reading this book."

For those currently enrolled, there are resource's available, that will help you obtain funding. There is an abundance of opportunity to receive financial aid, grants, and/or scholarships. The next question, you may be asking, is how do I obtain those funds for college?

To my girls in elementary through middle school. Pick a sport and get good at it. Work at it night and day. If you are already involved in a sport, awesomeness, you are one step ahead, which is always good.

To my young women who are not involved in a sport, it is not too late. You may ask, "Why did I request for you to pick a sport?" Playing sports and being good at it, equals scholarships for college.

I did not say you have to be the greatest, like Lisa Leslie or Simone Bile; being good is enough. Work at your sport night and day.

Second, do an excellent job in school; a great GPA equals scholarship. If you have low grades, have a conversation with your teacher, ask for ways to bring up your grades. Request a tutor or hours after school to meet with your teacher to go over assignments.

The help is there, however, a closed mouth never gets fed. If you are doing great in school, keep up the good work, there are scholarships for students who do well in school.

Student Internship

Experience teaches you to respect what you are up against. Student internships, provide an opportunity, to be introduced to your future career. It provides an opportunity for hands on experience. I would not suggest picking an internship just to receive credit.

It is best to research different organizations, that meet your interests. Find one that shares your same passion.

Student internships are important. It is a great way to get hands on experience, in any field you desire. It provides room for opportunity. You can pick anywhere to complete an internship.

Please do not limit yourself, the world is yours. There are millions of businesses and organizations to choose from, both corporate and nonprofit. It can be a field you are interested in, or a field you are not too sure about.

If you have settled on a field of interest, apply for an internship. You may apply for an internship at any state, federal, non-profit, or for-profit organization.

Not all internships are paid positions. Look for the paid internships first. You can work over the summer, and save money for your next semester of college.

Student internships are a way to get your foot in the door and to network. My first internship was at the Department of Youth Services (DYS) in Toledo, Ohio. I worked alongside a Juvenile Parole officer, Ms. Ashford.

Whatever she had to do that day, I rode along with her. Yes, a ride-along and it was an awesome experience. I learned what I loved and disliked about the job. Working at DYS provided the opportunity to network and find a second internship for my next semester of college.

My second internship was at Alvis House- OhioLink Corrections and Treatment Center, a half-way house serving men, women, and juveniles in Toledo.

The Senior Juvenile Parole officer made a call to the Director at the Halfway House. She informed the director about me and my desire to complete an internship for school and assisted with setting up an interview.

Working at the halfway house, I completed the same duties as their full-time workers. I completed security checks, urine analysis (drug drops), intake screenings, program orientation trainings, staff meetings, and I oversaw the day to day operations of the facility.

Interning at OhioLink was not a walk in the park and serious work. Guess what happened when I completed my internship? Since I was such an awesome student intern, learned quickly, and did everything I was supposed to do in a professional manner, I was hired as a Community Corrections Officer, two months after graduating, with my Degree in Criminal Justice.

Responsibility

You are responsible for your future. Yes, it is your parent's responsibility, to make sure you have the guidance and resources you need to succeed, but you are responsible for doing your best.

You are responsible, for what you do, with the hand you were dealt. You are responsible for what you do with the guidance, tools and resources given to you.

You are responsible for doing research on career fields that may interest you. Sometimes opportunities are offered at school. Some schools offer programs that help prepare you for your career. There are career preparatory high schools available, preparing students for their careers before graduating; cosmetology, auto mechanics and fashion design programs to name a few. There are also school organizations available; FBLA, DECA, and many more.

These programs provide opportunities of preparation. If you are thinking about these programs, or already involved, I am going to suggest you do the work necessary to succeed. You are responsible for your study habits. You are responsible for your successes; take control and do the work to be successful.

Yes, your parents can force you to study, read and finish your homework. Let's ponder on this, if your parents have to constantly remind you, all the time throughout high school, once you go away to college, who is going to remind you?

Who is going to teach you how to study, who is going to be your alarm clock? Your friends or your phone? You better think twice. The habits you take with you, are the same habits, you are going to have when you are in college as a young adult.

Goal Focused

It is important to start early being goal focused. Having goals allow you to stay organized and plan.

It is important to set small goals, ones that are obtainable. They will help create a desire to stay motivated, on your journey to achieving larger goals. Every day you should be working towards a goal.

Success is what you make it. Stop focusing so much on everything that is not going right, or everything that you have done wrong. Stop comparing yourself to other people's successes or stories.

Once you reach a goal, reward yourself. Learn to enjoy your success and reward yourself at the end.

I remember when I graduated with my Master's degree. Everyone around me was so ecstatic for me, but I was not. I did not have the awesome job I wanted, and I did not finish with the GPA I wanted.

But as I look back during the years of working towards my master's degree, it was challenging. I had many stressful days, some days I wanted to give up.

I learned to focus on the outcomes, not my current situation. I admire my passion to display exemplary behavior, never giving up. It is important to keep trying until you believe that you have given your all.

Although, I had many days I could not see through the storm, I pushed through and survived. I did it. I graduated. I was not at the top of my class, but I finished. The only thing that matters is that you get there and finish.

Do your homework. I was one of those high school students, who did not have to study hard for a test, and could pass it. I did not have to stay up hours studying the night before the test.

When you get to college, those study habits are not going to cut it. College exams can cover up to three or four chapters per test. Most exams are structured in sessions and covers well over four chapters. Then you have finals, at the end of each semester, which covers the entire first half of the book. I am not trying to overwhelm you; nonetheless, I believe in being prepared.

Currently, you may be in grade school or high school. Learn to develop study skills that work for you. Procrastination only causes stress.

Some may work well under stress, but why put your body through the fight or flight situation intentionally.

Do better now, so that you will be prepared, when you enroll in your first semester of college or trade program.

During my college experience, I spent many nights in the library. Find some study partners. In college, you will have your social friends and study groups. I would not suggest hanging out with the same crew all the time, learn from my experiences.

Many days, in the library, were social hours and we did not get much accomplished. Keep your study partners and social friends separated, you will be more productive.

Go- Getter

Anyone can set goals. A 'go getter' is a person who goes after life's goals. They do not sit around and wait for a hand out, or for someone else to show them the way.

The biggest step in being a 'go getter' is starting. We all have dreams and desires in our heart. Many individuals think it will cost too much, or it is not possible. I am here to remind you that the sky is not the limit. This universe is yours.

You have to go after what you want, be obedient and make sacrifices. You have favor, but the opportunity is not going to sit around and wait for you to move.

You must figure out what you need to do (plan), figure out the resources you will need (implement) and get it done (execute). Do not allow anything to get in your way, and do not allow anyone to hold you back.

Our Circle Is What Defines Us

"You are who you surround yourself with." Is a true statement. You know the saying, "Your team is only as strong as the weakest link."

There is no "I" in team. If someone on your team is struggling, you help the weaker link become strong, so the team will become stronger.

Surrounding yourself with good people, same analogy of staying connected to the vine, you have to surround yourself with people who are positive, mission driven, goal oriented, and self-sustaining.

I would not want to be around people who are not doing much with life, who are always complaining, cursing, and doing unproductive things. Why, because eventually that will become you. Hang around someone long enough, you eventually start talking and acting like them. It is true.

We have to learn to educate ourselves outside of our circles. We have to learn to expand our mind by expanding our circle.

If you are hanging around people that are not pushing you or vice versa, you should reevaluate your circle. Your circle should be adding growth to your development or impacting your life significantly.

It is not selfish to choose your circle. Not only are you in it for you, but to make your team better.

As Iyanla Vanzant says, *"I am not my sisters' keeper, I am my sister."*

≈≈≈≈≈≈

2 Timothy 3:1-7 (NIV).

¹ But mark this: There will be terrible times in the last days.

² People will be lovers of themselves, lovers of money, boastful, proud, abusive, disobedient to their parents, ungrateful, unholy,

³ without love, unforgiving, slanderous, without self-control, brutal, not lovers of the good,

⁴ treacherous, rash, conceited, lovers of pleasure rather than lovers of God —

⁵ having a form of godliness but denying its power. Have nothing to do with such people.

⁶ They are the kind who worm their way into homes and gain control over gullible women, who are loaded down with sins and are swayed by all kinds of evil desires,

⁷ always learning but never able to come to a knowledge of the truth.

≈≈≈≈≈≈

One Year Goals

_____
_____
_____
_____
_____
_____
_____

Two Year Goals

_____
_____
_____
_____
_____
_____
_____

Five-Year Goals

_____
_____
_____
_____
_____
_____
_____

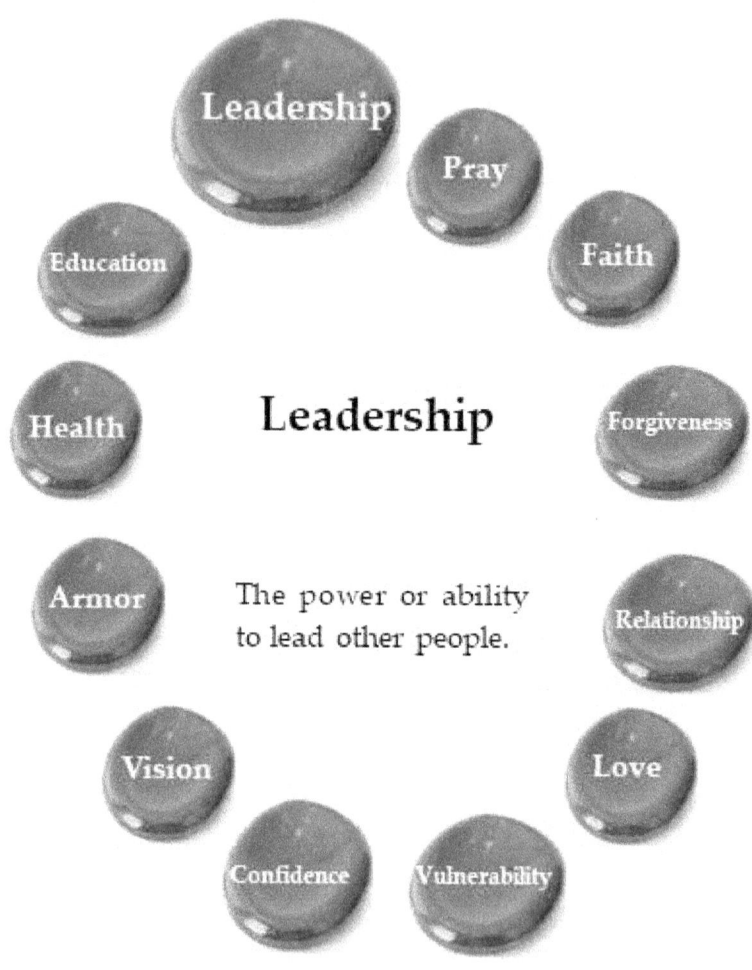

The Tool of Leadership

A leader strives to bring out the best in other people. A leader is assertive and can initiate. Leadership is the act of setting the right example for those who follow.

A leader is a visionary and a goal setter; striving to get the job done. Being a visionary, is having the ability to see the future. A leader has the ability to create innovative ideas and opportunities, to bring about change in the work place, the community, in schools, and businesses.

Many individuals set goals, but few do the work to achieve them. Goal setters do whatever it takes to get the job done. Excuses, what are they?

Leaders move past excuses. Excuses creates an opportunity to stop. Excuses are the problem of today —

- "But I was adopted."
- "But my dog ate my homework."
- "But I was a fatherless daughter."
- "But I was never loved."
- "But my parents abandoned me. "
- "But I was homeless."

Believe me I have a story just like you do. It is not about where I came from, it is about where I am going and how can I help you get there. It is not about what happened, but how you rise after it happens.

Learn to move past excuses and deal with the issue.

Having deep rooted issues, will hurt you and your ability to help others. Yes, you may learn many coping mechanisms, but if we fail to cope with the issues, we are only covering it up.

Why put a band aid on it, it is going to fall off and expose itself again? Why cover up something, when you can deal with it, as the leader you are, and never encounter it again.

When you acknowledge your situation- you are more than a conqueror. It will not go away forever, but when the issue arises again- you have learned different strategies to help you manage it differently. The devil likes to bring up things from our past. This time we are in control.

You will not have the same reaction, as in the past. You will not be angry but resilient.

Learning the word and meditating on it will help you develop strategies, to keep you grounded and provide strength during your healing. All issues stem from the enemy, God allows him to move on some things to test you. But it is for your greater good. Only good things come from the Lord.

≈≈≈≈≈≈

Joshua 23:14-16, (NIV).

14 Now I am about to go the way of all the earth. You know with all your heart and soul that not one of all the good promises the LORD your God gave you has failed. Every promise has been fulfilled; not one has failed.

15 But just as all the good things the LORD your God has promised you have come to you, so he will bring on you all the evil things he has threatened, until the LORD your God has destroyed you from this good land he has given you.

16 If you violate the covenant of the LORD your God, which he commanded you, and go and serve other gods and bow down to them, the LORD's anger will burn against you, and you will quickly perish from the good land he has given you.

≈≈≈≈≈≈

We all go through tests to gain the skills for future success, as a leader and a champion. If everything is given to you without working for it, you would probably be the most arrogant, ego centered leader.

Remember do not try to fix all your issues yourself; there is help. Go to counseling and talk to God. Ask for healing and deliverance from all things.

≈≈≈≈≈≈

Isaiah 58:8, (NIV).

8 Then your light will break forth like the dawn, and your healing will quickly appear; then your righteousness will go before you, and the glory of the LORD will be your rear guard.

≈≈≈≈≈≈

Deal with your pain, so you will be able to solve tomorrow's problems. There are professionals for a reason. Sometimes a situation is out of our control. Learn to use your resources and seek the help you need to be a better leader. You are the leader of your own empire. Your empire will fail or succeed, which do you prefer?

A leader is a person who works to be effective and efficient without being told what to do. A leader works alone and as a team player. A leader's job is not to do it by him or herself, but to inspire others to be better.

An importance part of leadership is knowing you do not have to have all the answers. A leader is always seeking new opportunities for growth and personal development. A leader is never stagnated.

We refer to many people as a BOSS, however a boss without leadership skills will be an ineffective boss.

Know the difference. A boss with ineffective leadership will have poor communication skills, never work alongside his or her employees, and most likely have a team of people behind them that resent them and never follows them. Who really wants to be a BOSS?

Great leaders are great, communicators. They know what to say and how to say it.

A great leader leads by example, building tomorrows leaders. Leaders demonstrate what's possible and creates the path to succeed. Being a leader may not come easy, but starting with self-development is the first step in being a great leader. As John Wooden stated, "the most powerful leadership tool you have is your own personal example."

≈≈≈≈≈≈

John 13:14-17, (NIV).

14 Now that I, your Lord and Teacher, have washed your feet, you also should wash one another's feet.

15 I have set you an example that you should do as I have done for you.

16 Very truly I tell you, no servant is greater than his master, nor is a messenger greater than the one who sent him.

17 Now that you know these things, you will be blessed if you do them.

≈≈≈≈≈≈

What are some characteristic of a great leader?

Scriptures

Scriptures on Prayer. (NIV), (KJV)
- And all things, whatsoever ye shall ask in prayer, believing, ye shall receive (Matthew 21:22). (KJV)
- Then you will call on me and come and pray to me, and I will listen to you (Jeremiah 29:12). (KJV)
- You will pray to him, and he will hear you, and you will fulfill your vows. (Job 22:27). (NIV)
- Therefore, I tell you, whatever you ask for in prayer, believe that you have received it, and it will be yours (Mark 11:24). (NIV)
- I call on you, my God, for you will answer me; turn your ear to me and hear my prayer (Psalm 17:6). (NIV)
- May my prayers be set before you like incense; may the lifting up of my hands be like the evening sacrifice (Psalm 141:2). (NIV)
- Be joyful in hope, patient in affliction, faithful in prayer (Romans 12:12). (NIV)
- The LORD is near to all who call on him, to all who call on him in truth (Psalms 145:18). (NIV)
- Pray continually (1 Thessalonians 5:17). (NIV)

Scriptures on Faith
- Behold, his soul which is lifted up is not upright in him; but the just shall live by his faith (Habakkuk 2:4). (KJV)
- Be not ye therefore like unto them: for your Father knoweth what things ye have need of, before ye ask him (Matthew 6:8). (KJV)

- And Jesus said unto them, Because of your unbelief: for verily I say unto you, If ye have faith as a grain of mustard seed, ye shall say unto this mountain, Remove hence to yonder place; and it shall remove; and nothing shall be impossible unto you (Matthew 17:20). (KJV)
- And he said unto them, Why, are ye so fearful? How is it that ye have no faith? (Mark 4:40). (KJV)
- For we walk by faith, not by sight: (2 Corinthians 5:7). (KJV)
- Remembering without ceasing your work of faith, and labor of love, and patience of hope in our Lord Jesus Christ, in the sight of God and our Father (Thessalonians 1:3). (KJV)
- I have fought a good fight, I have finished my course, I have kept the faith: (2 Timothy 4:7). (KJV)
- Let us draw near with a true heart in full assurance of faith, having our hearts sprinkled from an evil conscience, and our bodies washed with pure water (Hebrew 10:22). (KJV)
- Now faith is the substance of things hoped for, the evidence of things not seen (Hebrew 11:1). (KJV)
- But without faith it is impossible to please him (God); for he that cometh to God must believe that he is, and that he is a rewarder of them that diligently seek him (Hebrew 11: 6). (KJV)
- Knowing this, that the trying of your faith worketh patience (James 1:3). (KJV)

Scriptures on Forgiveness
- Bear with each other and forgive one another if any of you has a grievance against someone. Forgive as the Lord forgave you (Colossians 3.13). (NIV)
- But if you do not forgive others their sins, your Father will not forgive your sins (Matthew 6:15). (NIV)

- Get rid of all bitterness, rage and anger, brawling and slander, along with every form of malice. Be kind and compassionate to one another, forgiving each other, just as in Christ God forgave you (Ephesians 4:31-32). (NIV)
- The Lord our God is merciful and forgiving, even though we have rebelled against him; (Daniel 9:9). (NIV)
- "And when you stand praying, if you hold anything against anyone, forgive them, so that your Father in heaven may forgive you your sins." (Mark 11:25). (NIV).

Scriptures on Relationship

- One who has unreliable friends soon comes to ruin, but there is a friend who sticks closer than a brother (Proverbs 18:24). (NIV)
- Listen to advice and accept discipline and at the end you will be counted among the wise (Proverbs 19:20). (NIV)
- Make no friendships with an angry man; and with a furious man thou shalt not go: Lest thou learn his ways, and get a snare to thy soul. (Proverbs 22:24-25). (KJV)
- Make every effort to keep the unity of the Spirit through the bond of peace (Ephesians 4:3). (NIV)

Scriptures on Love

- But I say unto you, love your enemies, bless them that curse you, and do good to them that hate you, and pray for them which despitefully use you, and persecute you; (Matthew 5:44). (KJV)
- Be completely humble and gentle; be patient, bearing with one another in love (Ephesians 4:2). (KJV)
- Honour thy father and thy mother: and, thy shalt love the neighbor as thyself (Matthew 19:19). (KJV)

- Jesus answered and said unto him, If a man love me, he will keep my words: and my Father will love him, and we will come unto him, and make our abode with him (John 14:23). (KJV)
- As the Father hath loved me, so have I loved you: continue ye in my love (St. John 15:9). (KJV)
- These things I command you, that ye love one another (John 15:17). (KJV)
- That Christ may dwell in your hearts by faith; that ye, being rooted and grounded in love (Ephesians 3:17). (KJV)

Scriptures on Vulnerability
- We have spoken freely to you, Corinthians; our heart is wide open. You are not restricted by us, but you are restricted in your own affections. In return (I speak as to children) widen your hearts also (2 Corinthians 6:11-13). (NIV)
- But I say unto you which hear, love your enemies, do good to them which hate you, Blessed them that curse you, and pray for them which despitefully use your (Luke 6:27-28). (KJV)
- Confess your faults one to another, and pray on for another, that ye may be healed. The effectual fervent prayer of a righteous man availeth much (James 5:16). (KJV)
- A tranquil heart gives life to the flesh, but envy makes the bones rot (Proverbs 14:30). (NIV)
- Then Peter came up and said to him, "Lord, how often will my brother sin against me, and I forgive him? As many as seven times?" Jesus said to him, "I do not say to you seven times, but seventy times seven (Matthew 18:21-22). (KJV)
- But he said to me, "My grace is sufficient for you, for my power is made perfect in weakness." Therefore I will boast all the more gladly about my weaknesses, so that Christ's

power may rest on me. 10 That is why, for Christ's sake, I delight in weaknesses, in insults, in hardships, in persecutions, in difficulties. For when I am weak, then I am strong. (2 Corinthians 12:9-10). (NIV)

Scriptures on Confidence
- In whom we have boldness and access with confidence by the faith of Him. Wherefore I desire that ye faint not at my tribulations for you, which is your glory (Ephesians 3:12-13). (KJV)
- I can do all this through him who gives me strength (Philippians 4:13). (NIV)
- Such confidence we have through Christ before God (2 Corinthians 3:4). (NIV)

Scriptures on Vision
- Where there is no vision, the people perish: but he that keepeth the law, happy is he (Proverbs 29:18). (KJV)
- And it shall come to pass afterward, that I will pour out my spirit upon all flesh; and your sons and your daughters shall prophesy, your old men shall dream dreams, your young men shall see visons: (Joel 2:28). (KJV)
- Saying, Father, if thou be willing, remove this cup from me: nevertheless, not my will, but thine, be done (Luke 22:42). (KJV)

Scriptures on Armor
- Above all, taking the shield of faith wherewith ye shall be able to quench all the fiery darts of the wicked (Ephesians 6:16). (KJV)
- But let us, who are of the day, be sober, putting on the breastplate of faith and love, and for and helmet, the hope of salvation (1 Thessalonians 5:8). (KJV)

Scriptures on Health
- Casting all your anxiety on him because he cares for you (1 Peter 5:7). (KJV)
- For I will restore health unto thee, and I will heal thee of thy wounds, saith the LORD; because they called thee an Outcast, saying, this is Zion, whom no man seeketh after (Jeremiah 30:17). (KJV)

Scriptures on Education
- He that walketh with wise men shall be wise: but a companion of fools shall be destroyed (Proverbs 13:20). (KJV)
- If any of you lack wisdom, let him ask of God, that giveth to all men liberally, and upbraideth not; and it shall be given him (James 1: 5). (KJV)
- Wisdom resteth in the heart of him that hath understanding: but that which is in the midst of fools is made known (Proverbs 14:33). (KJV)

Scriptures on Leadership
- Do to others as you would have them do to you (Luke 6:31). (NIV)
- Humble yourselves before the Lord, and he will lift you up (James 4:10). (NIV)
- Do nothing out of selfish ambition or vain conceit. Rather, in humility value others above yourselves (Philippians 2:3). (NIV)
- Don't let anyone look down on you because you are young, but set an example for the believers in speech, in conduct, in love, in faith and in purity (1 Timothy 4:12). NIV)

Favorite Scriptures

Favorite Scriptures

Favorite Scriptures

Favorite Scriptures

About the Author

Estitia Stone's career experience specializing in youth development, stemmed from group homes, scouts, summer camps, community corrections and case management.

She admires the powerful platform young women have and strives to make sure all girls have essential tools necessary to be the best they can be in life. Estitia gives back to the community through volunteer work and community service.

Estitia is the founder of Girls Circle Youth Development Inc. and look forward to serving many communities – ensuring success in girls lives and career path by closing gaps between youth development and career readiness.

email: info@estitiastone.com
Facebook: estitiastone
Instagram: _estitia
website: www.estitiastone.com
ISBN: 978-0-692-94716-6

Reference

Hacker. (2011). Merriam-Webster.com. Retrieved March 13, 2017, from: https://www.merriam-ebster.com/dictionary/hacker

NAMI. (n.d.). Retrieved March 13, 2017, from: http://www.nami.org/Learn-More/Mental-Health-By-the-Numbers

Bible Study Tools. (n.d.) Retrieved from: http://www.biblestudytools.com

www.ingramcontent.com/pod-product-compliance
Lightning Source LLC
Chambersburg PA
CBHW050641160426
43194CB00010B/1762